WHY HAVEN'T I *Received Healing?*

REV PABLO AROCHA

ISBN: 979-8-89419-265-9 (sc)
ISBN: 979-8-89419-266-6 (hc)
ISBN: 979-8-89419-267-3 (e)

One Galleria Blvd., Suite 1900, Metairie, LA 70001
(504) 702-6708

Dedication

This first edition of the book was never intended to be explained in a storytelling fashion but to be shared in the form of individual topics from the Book of Genesis to the Book of Revelation in order to obtain the completed intent.

All these topics are not presented in their totality, but the reader may gain a completed overview of its original intent, which is God's common union with humanity, God's best for humanity, God's ultimate wellness for humanity, and ultimately having a healthy family and bride to rapture.

I would like to dedicate this book to every person around the world who is in desperate need of a touch from God.

I would also like to dedicate this book to all the heartbroken people around the world.

I would also like to dedicate this book to the lonely, to the sick, to the hopeless, to the weary, and to the forsaken in the hospitals around the world.

I would also like to dedicate this book to every human being that is in such a need for a miracle.

I want to dedicate this to every mom and dad who has a child in bed, who has a child in a hospital, and who is pleading with our heavenly Father for a miracle.

To every person who has lost their hope in a God who heals and sets people free.

To every person who needs to be reconciled with God.

To every brother and sister in the Lord who is sick in bed or is dying with an incurable disease.

To every person who did not believe in Jesus Christ and through the reading of this book, they have developed a relationship with God through Jesus Christ.

I would also like to dedicate this book to the many thousands of people who have been prayed for by ministers, evangelists, and every other prayer made known to man, and they are still sick.

I would also like to dedicate it to you, the reader, that after receiving a supernatural touch from God, you would be inspired to get a copy of this book and give it to someone or take one to somebody in a hospital somewhere, as a seed sowed in someone else.

Contents

The Evangelist's Story 1
Why Haven't I Received Healing? 5
Acknowledgements 7
Introduction 9

1. God's creation 9
2. Purpose of creation 10
3. God gave man a mission 10
4. God gave man a helper 11
5. Disobedience entered the garden 11
6. The curse upon all created 13
7. The curse causes alienation from God 13
8. Cain the murderer 14
9. Man's wickedness 15
10. Promise of covenant 16
11. God blessed Noah 19
12. God's covenant with Noah 19

13. The rainbow, God's covenant with Noah and man 19
14. Descendants of Noah 20
15. The Tower of Babel 21
16. The God of covenant...............................21
17. Abraham prays for Sodom, And Gomorrah 23
18. God tests Abraham's faith...........................25
19. Birth of Esau and Jacob 26
20. And Passover was instituted by God 30
21. The Ten Commandments are given 30
22. Why don't I get healed? 31
23. A thought of being under a generational curse.............32
24. God's name, God is a healer 34
25. God's word is God's covenant, God's commitment. 34
26. God's word is settled in heaven 35
27. God's word is a lamp and a light 36
28. God's word gives light and understanding................37
29. God's desire, man's choice 37
30. What is healing? It's a change of health with divine help.....39
31. Examples of Jesus delivering and healing the afflicted.......44
32. A new scenario with a different requirement 46
33. Some sickness could be the result of sin 47
34. Why permit sickness? 53
35. Examples of healing done through Peter and Paul..........56
36. God-given authority 59
37. This commission has been given and ordered by God.......62
38. What must I do to get healed?.........................63

39. Number 1, not understanding the "substitution," death, burial, and resurrection of our Lord Jesus Christ on our behalf. 66

40. Number 2, not understanding the "mediation" and "propitiation" between God and man. 68

41. Number 3, not knowing "justification." .70

42. Number 4, not knowing there is a new law called "the law of faith." 73

43. Number 5, not honoring God's anointed 80

44. Number 6, disregarding grace and going back to tradition. . .81

45. Number 7, not walking in love, two new commandments . . .86

46. Number 8, taking the Lord's supper in an unworthy manner.. 91

47. Number 9, dishonoring God, wrath of God revealed 93

48. Number 10, disobedience to God's word and unforgiveness. 102

49. (12) Natural reasons why people haven't received their healing.. 108

50. (13) Not knowing our identity in Christ (we are somebody). 110

51. (14) Prayer the key to access 124

52. (15) Not knowing how to enter God's Holy of Holies (through prayer) 127

About the Author 137

The Evangelist's Story

Rev. Pablo Arocha, an evangelist and ordained by Rev. Charles Quinn from Trinity Agape Church, while inside the Trinity Broadcasting Network Channel 45 in Miami, Florida, and nine other Pentecostal preachers, after laying hands on me, ordained me into the full-time ministry in 1989.

Also, in 1985, I received ordination licenses from the United Christian Church and Ministerial Association through 1989. From 1983 to 1985, I received some formal education from Miami Christian College. I am the founder and president of He Cares Ministries Inc. and the HCM publications.

I have had the privilege of preaching the uncompromising full gospel of the Lord Jesus Christ in the Miami-Dade county jails for almost fifteen years, with untold results of lives being turned around, eyes being opened, people being delivered from the occult, marriages being restored, sentences being reduced, and then finally the HCH prevention program being open to the public.

There we preached the holy Word of God to more than a hundred people, including the family members of the prisoners from the Dade County Jail, getting whole families saved. We also had a food bank, where we fed over ninety-two thousand people after Hurricane Andrew.

We then opened the HCH Drug Rehabilitation Center, where we housed twenty-four drug addicts and some homeless, which was licensed by the State of Florida and financed in part by Dade County

Commission Board. And for seven years, we had the privilege of seeing our clients turn around for the glory of God.

And while all this was going on, we were having evangelistic meetings in some of the local churches, bringing revival, praying for the sick, and seeing them recover.

Some testimonials of healings being performed by God Almighty in the name of Jesus, and by the power of the Holy Spirit found in 1 Corinthians 12:4–18 verse 9, to another faith by the same spirit, and to another gift of healing by the one spirit.

In these evangelistic meetings, people came to the front asking to be healed by the power of God, and according to James 5:14–15, "Is anyone among you sick? Let them call for the elders of the church, and let them pray over him, anointing him with oil in the name of the Lord; and the prayer offered in faith will restore the one who is sick, and the Lord will raise him up, and if he has committed sins, they will be forgiven him."

So I would take out a bottle of oil, anoint the person, and say the prayer of faith in the name of Jesus, and they would all recover.

I have prayed for creative miracles for people's eyes, and they received them.

I have prayed for people bleeding through their nipples, and they have been healed.

I have prayed for people with AIDS, and they have been completely delivered.

I have prayed for a person in coma, and God has raised him up and healed him.

I have prayed for people with cancer, and God has completely healed them.

I have prayed for people dying on their deathbeds inside hospitals, and I have wept to God for them in Jesus's name, and God has restored their lives with fifteen extra years.

I have prayed for prisoners who couldn't read the Bible because they had no glasses, and God restored their eyesight perfectly.

I have literally prayed for hundreds, if not thousands, of people to be set free from all occult activity, and God has miraculously set them free and saved them by the power of the Holy Spirit.

I have prayed for people with incurable blood diseases, and God Almighty has made them well.

So, friend, or my brother and my sister reading this book, this is not a fairytale. This is the story of my life, and I have other untold stories and many other miracles and many more deliverances that I could share with you all, but for the sake of time, this is all for now.

After studying the life and ministry of Aimee Semple McPherson, Mr. Jack Cole, Mr. T. L. Osborn, Mr. Oral Roberts, Mr. R. W. Schambach, Mr. A. A. Allen, Mr. William Seymour, Mr. John Alexander Dowie, Mr. Smith Wigglesworth, Mr. Kenneth E. Hagin, Mrs. Katherine Kuhlman, Mr. William Branham, and Mr. Benny Hinn.

All of them intrigued me a lot by saying from the pulpit that when they get to heaven, they are going to ask the Lord why in so many of their crusades, only a handful of people were healed by the power of God Almighty and the rest of them went home in their wheelchairs and on their deathbeds.

Now, this book that I just wrote, it's not as complete and detailed as I would have liked it. After all, I don't consider myself an author, but I have given ten major Biblical reasons why people don't get healed and some personal egotistical natural reasons why they don't want to be healed, and I have found in the scriptures that there are more reasons why people don't get healed. But I did not have the time to write them. Well, perhaps in my next volume.

What is important is that my heart cries out to God when I see the needy, the heartbroken, the unsaved, and also the sick. When God told me to write this book almost fifteen years ago, I ran from the idea because of the responsibility behind it and the lack of financial resources.

I have poured out my heart to the best of my ability with so little time, and my prayers are that the God of Abraham, Isaac, and Jacob, the Father of our Lord Jesus Christ, will set you free from the crown of your head to the soles of your feet and that God's best will be poured in your life, in your spirit, soul, and body. May God richly bless you and everyone reading this book, in Jesus's name, amen.

Why Haven't I Received Healing?

In order to understand that question, you must understand God's original intent in creation. Everything that God taught us in His Word is that He doesn't do something or nothing without a purpose. Everything that God does has a purpose and a reason behind it. Healing is in the atonement, as written in the Old and New Testament covenants for the believer.

Acknowledgements

As with any major endeavor, it takes a great team of people to inspire, to motivate, and to be an intricate part in some way, shape, or form in the production of such a book.

I want to give my sincere thanks for their hard work and untiring commitment to the following:

My daughter, Annette Arocha, without whose love and unwavering commitment to my life, this book would not have been possible.

Pablo M. Arocha, who, in times of need, has proven to be helpful.

Mr. Miguel Palacios, for being unafraid to speak his mind and for being a good brother in Christ.

Rev. Bobby Rosario, for his love, compassion, caring, and loving spirit.

Fatih, owner and general manager of Lombardy's Rest, Bay side, for his generous contribution and support.

Carlos Arocha, my younger brother, an engineer and a committed hard worker.

Marta Canals, my sister, for her love and devoted hard work.

Francisco Arocha, a very tough businessman and partial contributor.

Mr. Bryant Miller, a brother in Christ and a partial supporter.

Ms. Susan Weeks, for her courage, dedication, and support.

Mr. Paul and Jan Crouch, for their inspiration through Christian television for the last forty years through excellent Christian programming.

Dr. Mike Murdock, for his many inspirational books and spiritual insight into the Holy Bible.

Mr. Augusto Colorado, for his total commitment to us in every area of this project.

And to the most important person, God the Holy Spirit, who inspired, revealed, illuminated, and spoke to my heart about the great need there is in the body of Christ. To God be the glory.

Introduction

God's creation

Genesis 1:26–27 states,

> **And God said, let us make man in our image, after our likeness; let them have dominion over the fish of the sea, and over the fowl of the air, and over the cattle, and over all the earth, and over every creeping thing that creeps upon the earth. So God created man in his own image, in the image of God created he him; male and female created he them.**

As we can see in these paragraphs, man was made in God's own image. God is an eternal spirit. He made man out of the dust of the ground and breathed into his nostrils the breath of life, and man became a living soul, having fellowship vertically with God and horizontally with his wife. Man was made to live forever. He was going to be the god of this world, perfect and sinless, with a common union with his Creator and daily fellowship in the cool of the day in the Garden of Eden. The soul that God put in man gives him the right to choose; he has emotions, and he stores knowledge. Man became spirit, soul, and body, a free moral agent.

Purpose of creation

Genesis 1:28 states,

> **And God blessed them, and God said unto them, be fruitful, and multiply, and replenish the earth, and subdue it; and have dominion over the fish of the sea, and over the fowl of the air, and over every living thing that moves upon the earth.**

As we can see from this paragraph on the purpose of creation, the creation of man was so that he would have dominion over the earth, over everything that crept on the earth and over every living creature on the earth. Man was perfect in his spirit, perfect in his soul, and perfect in his body. His body was perfect. There was no sin in his body, so he was going to live forever.

God gave man a mission

Genesis 2:19–20 states,

> **And out of the ground the Lord God formed every beast of the field, and every fowl of the air; and brought them onto Adam to see what he would call them; and whatsoever Adam called every living creature, that was the name thereof. And Adam gave names to all the cattle, and to the fowl of the air, and to every beast of the field; but for Adam there was not found an help meet for him.**

Adam was given a job. His mission in life was to name the animals. He had a job to accomplish, and he was alone without a helper.

God gave man a helper

Genesis 2:21–23 states,

> **And the Lord God caused a deep sleep to fall upon Adam, and he slept; and he took one of his ribs, and closed up the flesh instead thereof; and the rib, which the Lord God had taken from man, made he a woman and brought her unto the man. And Adam said this is now bone of my bones, and flesh of my flesh; she shall be called woman, because she was taken out of man.**

From these paragraphs, we see God making a helper for man, a helpmeet, someone to give him moral support, to be by his side, to give him the necessary help on his mission, and to also keep him company while carrying out his mission.

Why did God form the woman out of his left rib and not from his head or from his feet?

God made her from the left rib on the side of the heart so he would cherish her and keep her by his side—not from the head so she would not lord over him and not from the feet so he would not step over her—and so that together they would move forward side by side in accomplishing the mission that God gave to man.

Disobedience entered the garden

Genesis 3:1–13 states,

> **Now the serpent was smarter than any beast of the field which the Lord God had made. And he said unto the woman, yeah, has God said, you shall not eat of every tree of the garden? And the woman said unto the serpent, we may eat of the fruit of the trees of the garden; but of the fruit of the tree which is in**

the midst of the garden, God hath said you shall not eat of it, neither shall ye touch it, lest ye die. And the serpent said unto the woman, ye shall not surely die. For God doth know that in the day you eat there off, then your eyes shall be opened, and ye shall be as gods, knowing good and evil. And when the woman saw that the tree was good for food, and that it was pleasant to the eyes, and a tree to be desired to make one wise, she took of the fruit thereof, and did eat, and gave also unto her husband with her; and he did eat. And the eyes of them both were opened, and they knew that they were naked; and they sewed fig leaves together, and made themselves aprons. And they heard the voice of the Lord God walking in the garden in the cool of the day; and Adam and his wife hid themselves from the presence of the Lord God amongst the trees of the garden. And the Lord God called on to Adam and said unto him, where art thou? And he said, I heard thy voice in the garden, and I was afraid, because I was naked; and I hid myself. And he said, who told thee that thou wast naked? Hast thou eaten of the tree, whereof I commanded thee that thou shouldest not eat? And the man said, the woman whom thou gave to me, she gave me of the tree, and I did eat. And the Lord God said unto the woman, what is this that thou has done? And the woman said, The serpent lied to me, and I did eat.

In this paragraph, we see the sin of omission, which is forgetfulness, carelessness, and disobedience. The sin of omission, which carries these characteristics, will always lead us to the sin of commission, which will take us to the act of doing something God told us not to do, which always keeps us alienated from our heavenly Father and Maker.

The curse upon all created

Genesis 3:14–21 states,

> **And the Lord God said unto the serpent, because thou hast done this, thou art cursed above all cattle, and above every beast of the field; upon thy belly shalt thou go, and dust shalt thou eat all the days of thy life. And I will put enmity between thee and the woman, and between thy seed and her seed; it shall bruise thy head, and thou shall bruise his heel. Unto the woman he said, I will greatly multiply thy sorrow and thy conception; in sorrow thou shall bring forth children; and thy desire shall be to thy husband, and he shall rule over thee. And unto Adam he said, because thou has hearkened unto the voice of thy wife, and hast eaten of the tree, of which I commanded thee, saying, thou shall not eat of it; cursed is the ground for thy sake; in sorrow shall thou eat of it all the days of thy life; Thorns also and thistles shall it bring forth to thee; and thou shall eat the herb of the field; In the sweat of thy face shalt thou eat bread, till thou return unto the ground; for out of it was thou taken; for dust thou art, and unto dust shalt thou return. And Adam called his wife's name Eve; because she was the mother of all living. Unto Adam also and to his wife did the Lord God make coats of skins, and clothed them.**

The curse causes alienation from God

In Genesis 3:22–24, man lost his spiritual relationship with God. He can no longer communicate with God; he's pushed out of the garden. God and man break fellowship, and man now has a fallen, sinful body, which will grow old and ultimately die. Man becomes morally bankrupt and physically dead. Adam and Eve are now out of the garden. They start multiplying, and they have two children, Cain and Abel.

Cain the murderer

Genesis 4:8 states,

> **And Cain talked with Abel his brother: and it came to pass, when they were in the field that Cain rose up against Abel his brother, and slew him. And the Lord said unto Cain, where is Abel thy brother? And he said I know not am I my brother's keeper? And he said what have you done? The voice of thy brother's blood cries out on to me from the ground.**

We see the wages of sin here. We see the sinfulness of a fallen race even from the beginning with how they started to kill one another. Cain becomes a murderer. Cain becomes a liar. Cain becomes a deceiver. Cain becomes jealous. Cain becomes envious of his brother. Can you see the malice in Cain? Can you see the mistreatment of his brother?

We were going to live forever, but because of the curse, we are now dead in our sins and trespasses. Romans 3:23 says, "For the wages of sin is death, but the gift of God is eternal life through Jesus Christ our Lord."

Man needs redemption, but without the shedding of blood, there is no remission of sin. We are all descendants of Adam and Eve. We all have a fallen nature; no one can escape this fallen state. We are all sinners who need to be saved by grace, which is the gift of God.

Notice in these next teachings how the life expectancy of human beings became shorter and shorter.

Adam lived for 930 years. Seth, his third son, lived for 912 years, Enos for 905 years, Enos's son for 910 years, Maha for 895 years, Jared for 962 years, Enoch for 365 years, Methuselah for 969 years, and Lamech for 777 years. As you can see, from 969 years, as human beings became further and further away from God and became more and more morally corrupt and more and more alienated from God, they lived shorter and shorter lives.

Man's wickedness

Genesis 6:1–7 states,

> **As human beings began to multiply on the face of the earth, and daughters were born on to them, That the sons of God saw the daughters of men That they were fair; And they took them wives of all which they chose. And the Lord said, my spirit shall not always strive with man, for that he also is flesh: Yet his days shall be 120 years.**

As we can see in these paragraphs, God cuts the human beings' life span from 969 years to 120. Only one-third of the original years were given to man as man becomes more and more wicked, more and more alienated, more and more an idolater, and further and further away from God. His wickedness was great on earth that every imagination of the thoughts of his heart was only evil continually.

> **God repented from ever making man, and he grieved him in his heart. And the Lord said, I will destroy man whom I have created from the face of the earth; both men, and beast, and the creeping thing, and the fowls of the air; for it repented me that I have made them.**

Can you believe how sorry God must've been? He was so grieved in his heart that he actually repented for making human beings in his image and likeness, created for fellowship, common union, and relationship. Only one family found favor in the eyes of God, and that was Noah's family.

Noah found grace in the eyes of the Lord. Genesis 8:8 states,

> **These are the generations of Noah: Noah was a just man and perfect in his generations, and Noah walked with God. And Noah begat three sons, Shem, Ham, and Japheth. This is where all humans came from. And the earth was corrupt before God, and the earth was filled with violence. And God looked upon the earth, and behold, it was corrupt; for all flesh had corrupted its way upon the earth. And God said unto Noah, the end all of all flesh is come before me; for the earth is filled with violence through them; and, behold, I will destroy them with the earth.**

And as you can see, my friend, God's wrath came upon human beings because of their violence, because of their corruption, because of their wickedness. That was why he needed to redeem them.

Some people don't get healed because they don't understand the love, mercy, and judgment of God. It was never God's intention for his created beings to be alienated from him. It was the corruption found in man that alienated himself from God. God's original intent was to have fellowship and a common union with human beings and to make sure they were all healthy, as we can see in Genesis 6:14. God said to Noah to make himself an ark. God was about to save them. God was about to redeem them. God was about to protect the only family on the face of the earth that truly found favor with him.

Promise of covenant

Genesis 6:18 states,

> **But I will establish my covenant with you; and you shall enter the ark-you and your sons and your wife, and your sons' wives with you.**

He destroyed all, but here we see the promise of the covenant with human beings. Even after the flood, even after human beings, God still made a covenant with Noah that he would never flood the earth with water again.

In Genesis 7:1, it states,

> **And the Lord said unto Noah come thou and all thy house into the ark; for thee have I seen righteous before me in this generation.**

In verses 11–13, it states,

> **In the 600 year of Noah's life, this 17th day of the month, the same day were all the fountains of the great deep broken up, and the windows of heaven were opened in the second month. And the rain was upon the earth 40 days and 40 nights. In the selfsame day enter Noah and his three sons and their wives into the ark.**

In verse 18, it states,

> **And the waters prevailed, and were increased greatly upon the earth; and the ark went upon the face of the waters.**

From these paragraphs, we see how God's mercy upon Noah and his family prevailed by having Noah build an ark and saving his entire family, but all the other human beings on the face of the planet were all dead. No other human being was alive on the planet, only Noah and his eight family members. Despite God's pain in his heart, he was still a merciful, loving, compassionate, gentle, and caring heavenly Father. He is a holy God and cannot permit sin.

Genesis 8:1 states,

> **And God remembered Noah and every living thing, and all the cattle that were with him in the ark: and God made a wind to pass over the earth, and the waters receded.**

Verse 6 states,

> **And the ark rested in the seventh month, on the 17th day of the month, upon the mountains of Ararat.**

By the way, that mountain is in the country of Turkey.

Verses 15–16 states,

> **And God spake unto Noah saying, Go forth out of the ark, thou and thy wife, and thy sons and thy sons wives with thee.**

God saves them and then tells them to leave the ark.

Verse 20 states,

> **And Noah built an altar on to the Lord; took of every clean beast, and of every clean fowl, and offered burnt offerings on the altar.**

Notice what people do after God saves them. Noah realized he had just been saved from the wrath of a holy God, and he went ahead to build an altar of sacrifice unto his Savior. Noah had to be a very grateful, appreciative, and thankful individual, the only one God chose from all the other human beings only because he obeyed God's laws and found favor in the eyes of God.

God blessed Noah

Genesis 9:1 states,

> **And God blessed Noah and his sons, and said unto them, be fruitful, and multiply, and replenish the earth.**

God's covenant with Noah

Genesis 9:8–11 states,

> **And God spake unto Noah and to his sons with him, saying, And I, behold, I establish my covenant with you, and with your seed after you; And with every living creature that is with you, of the fowl, of the cattle, and of every beast of the earth with you; from all that go out of the ark, to every beast of the earth. I will establish my covenant with you, neither shall all flesh be cut off any more by the waters of a flood; neither shall there anymore be a flood to destroy the earth.**

The rainbow, God's covenant with Noah and man

Genesis 9:12–17 states,

> **And God said, this is the token of the covenant which I make between me and you and every living creature that is with you, for perpetual generations. I do set my bow in the cloud, and it shall be for a token of the covenant between me and the earth. And it shall come to pass, when I bring a cloud over the earth, that the bow shall be seen in the cloud: And I will remember**

> **my covenant, which is between me and you and every living creature of all flesh; and the waters shall no more become a flood to destroy all flesh. And the bow shall be in the cloud; and I will look upon it, that I may remember the everlasting covenant between God and every living creature of all flesh that is upon the earth. And God said unto Noah this is the token of the covenant, which I have established between me and all flesh that is upon the earth.**

To this day, every time it rains and we see a beautiful rainbow, remember that our heavenly Father keeps his word and his covenant in the sky and that we all should be grateful.

Now let's recap: a God of holiness, a God of warning, a God of judgments, a God of love, a God of provision, a God of promise, and a God of covenant.

Descendants of Noah

Genesis 10:32 states,

> **These are the families of the sons of Noah, according to their genealogies, by their nations; and out of these the nations were separated on the earth after the flood.**

In Genesis 11:10–26, we see the descendants of Shem. Shem lived for 500 years, and he had a son, and he lived for 403 years. He had a son, and he lived for 403 years, and this son had another son, and he lived for 430 years, and another son lived for 209 years, and another son who lived for 207 years, and another son who lived for only 200 years, and another son who lived for only 119 years, and Abraham's father lived only 205 years.

It is important to understand why I'm doing this. I am showing you that as human beings progressed and became knowledgeable about sin, rebellion, and disobedience, the age span became shorter and shorter despite the fact that Noah lived for 950 years. That's found in Genesis 9:29.

The Tower of Babel

Genesis 11:1 states,

> **And the whole earth was of one language, and of one speech.**

As we can see from the following verses all the way down to verse 9, verse 5, they try to build a city and a tower, whose top may reach the heavens; and let us make us a name, lest we be scattered abroad upon the face of the whole earth.

And in these verses, we see a new kind of sin, which is the sin of self-exaltation, the sin of pride, the sin of arrogance, and God had to come down and confuse their mind, confuse their language, and all the dialects of the world came out of this pride.

All the languages, all the peoples of the earth, and all the religions of the entire earth came out from this tower of Babel, from this particular rebellion.

The God of covenant

In Genesis 15:8, we see the God of Abraham, Isaac, and Jacob, making a covenant with Abraham, saying, **"To your descendants, I have given this land, from the river Egypt as far as the great river, the river Euphrates."**

Verses 19–21 mention the Kenites, Kenizzites, and Kadmonites; the Hittites, Perizzites, and Rephaites; and the Amorites, Canaanites, Girgashites, and Jebusites.

Notice in these verses how God not only made a covenant with Abraham but also gave him the land and dominion over the people that inhabited it.

Genesis 17:7–13 states,

> **And I will establish my covenant between me and thee and thy seed after thee in their generations for an everlasting covenant, to be a God unto thee, and to thy seed after thee. And I will give unto thee, and to thy seed after thee, the land where in thou art a stranger, all the land of Canaan, for an everlasting possession; and I will be there God. And God said unto Abraham, thou shall keep my covenant therefore, thou, and thy seed after thee in their generations. This is my covenant, which ye shall keep, between me and you and thy seed after thee; Every man child among you shall be circumcised. And you shall circumcise the flesh of your foreskin; and it shall be a token of the covenant between me and you. And he that is eight days old shall be circumcised among you, every man child in your generations, he that is born in the house, or bought with money of any stranger, which is not of thy seed. He that is born in thy house, and he that is bought with thy money, must needs be circumcised: and my covenant shall be in your flesh for an everlasting covenant.**

It is very important to understand that our heavenly Father is a God of covenant, that he made a physical covenant with Noah, made a physical covenant with Abraham, and did it by circumcising every single child that was in Abraham's home, the ones that were born out of him and also those that were bought with his money, and this particular circumcision was of the flesh. Our God is a God of signs and wonders, signs up in the sky and signs in the foreskin of the male Israeli children.

This new covenant in the flesh of the male children of Israel is important for us all to understand that it is an everlasting covenant. Everywhere on this planet, you see human beings making contracts, making commitments to one another, making marriage vows. And while everything is working okay, everybody's happy, everybody's together, everybody's united, when things start going wrong, contracts are destroyed, marriage vows are destroyed, relationships are destroyed, and everything falls apart.

We must understand that with human beings, things do fall apart because we have a fallen, sinful nature, and we are not eternal, as our heavenly Father is. We do have an eternal soul but a fallen human nature. All of us, at times, are inconsistent in our ways, thoughts, life, and behavior, but thank God that our heavenly Father is almighty, all-powerful, all-knowing, everywhere present, and he loves his children and wants to fellowship with them.

Aren't we happy we can depend on God Almighty, that we can depend on his promises, and that he will never leave us nor for sakes us? Just on those promises alone, we can be solid and secure.

Abraham prays for Sodom, And Gomorrah

In Genesis 18:23–33, we see Abraham pleading with God Almighty to be merciful to a city that was completely full of corruption and every sodomy imaginable to the human mind to the point where they wanted to have sex with God's three angels that came down to judge the city.

Can you believe how abominable this is? Three angels from heaven come to judge the city, and the morally corrupt human beings want to have sex with God's angels. How sick can this be? Do you know of anything more depraved than that?

Abraham's first petition to God was to spare the city if there were fifty righteous in it, and God said, "All right, I will not destroy the city if there are fifty righteous in it."

The second petition from Abraham to God: "Lord, if there be forty righteous in the city, will you not spare the city?" And God said, "All right, I will not destroy the city if there are forty righteous people in it."

The third petition from Abraham to God: "Lord, if there be thirty righteous in the city, will you spare the city?" And God said, "All right, I will spare the city if there are thirty righteous people in it."

The fourth petition from Abraham to God: "Lord, if there be twenty righteous in the city, will you spare the city?" And God said, "All right, I will spare the city if there are twenty righteous people in it."

And he said, "Oh, let not the Lord be angry, and I will speak yet but this once: if ten shall be found there."

And he answered, "I will not destroy it for the ten's sake."

In these verses, we see a loving, compassionate Abraham wanting to save an entire city from their complete destruction, pleading with God Almighty to spare the city and notice how God went from fifty to forty, from forty to thirty, from thirty to twenty, and from twenty to ten. You see the compassion and understanding of a loving heavenly Father. Some people don't understand our heavenly Father. Some people think he is a judge, but God has two major characteristics, a God of love and a God of judgment. He is not willing that any should perish but that all would come to repentance. It is impossible for man to live alienated and excommunicated from a holy heavenly Father and still live happily ever after without self-destruction.

In Genesis 19:12, Lot and his family flee from the city, and from verses 12 to 29, we see the complete message where God and his angels pass judgment upon Sodom and Gomorrah and burn it to the ground.

In Genesis 21:1–8, we see that God promises Abraham a son through Sarah and that he will call him Isaac.

In verses 9–16, we see Sarah and Abraham talking, and Sarah is telling Abraham to let go of Agar and her son, Ishmael, out into the wilderness because she does not want Ishmael to be an heir with Isaac in the family, so Abraham removes them from the camp even though it grieves him because Ishmael is his son and he loves him.

From verses 17 to 21, we see how God spares the lad, and he grows up and lives in the wilderness and becomes an archer, and his mother marries him with a woman out of Egypt and twelve princes, according to their nations, come from him (Genesis 25:12–18).

And as you can see, Ishmael is the father of all Arabs around the world. He is a descendant of Abraham, out of the loins of Abraham with Agar, his maid.

Can you see the loving mercies of our heavenly Father? Can you see how despite the fact that Ishmael was not the original child of Sarah, God still loved him, cared for him, and watched over him, making him a very huge, strong, and powerful nation?

God tests Abraham's faith

In Genesis 22:1–14, we read that after twenty-five years of waiting for Isaac, God now tells Abraham to sacrifice him on the altar as a burnt offering. That is a very tough instruction. God was testing Abraham's faith to see how loyal, faithful, and committed he was in obeying God's voice.

Verses 17–18 states,

> **That in blessing I will bless thee, and in multiplying I will multiply thy seed as the stars of the heaven, and as the sand which is upon the seashore; and thy seed shall possess the gate of his enemies. And in thy seed shall all the nations of the earth be blessed; because thou hast obeyed my voice. We must understand the generational blessing upon us, thanks to Abraham. And Jesus Christ.**

Now when we do a careful study of all the descendants of Abraham through the bloodline of Isaac, we will see that Jesus Christ of Nazareth, born of a virgin called Mary, and Joseph both came out of the loins of Abraham. Now this is in the natural course. Jesus Christ of Nazareth was God in person, one hundred percent God, one hundred percent man, with a sinless body. In Galatians 3:16–18, it states that through the bloodline of Isaac came Jesus, forty-two generations from Abraham to Jesus (Matthew 1:1–17).

More of Jesus Christ later. Let's continue with the chronological order of God's love, mercy, compassion, and covenant with the human race.

In Genesis 13:2, it states that Abraham was very rich in cattle and in silver. Now silver is a type of intelligence found in Proverbs 16:16, and gold, which is a type of wisdom, is also found in Proverbs 16:16.

In Romans 4:13, God promised Abraham the world.

In Galatians 3:14, God promised Abraham the Spirit.

In Genesis 25:7–11, God promised Abraham a long life, a good old age, no sickness, and an elderly life full of years.

In Genesis 23:6, the people considered him a prince.

In Genesis 17:5–9, God changed his name from Abram to Abraham. "Father of many nations have I made thee."

In Genesis 17:6, God multiplied him greatly and said, "I will establish my covenant with me and thee, and make thee exceedingly fruitful, and I will make nations of you, and kings shall come forth from you."

In verse 9, God said to Abraham, "Thou shall keep my covenant therefore, thou, and thy seed after thee in their generations."

It is vitally important that we keep understanding the promises of God to Abraham and his seed, which is Isaac, Jacob, and so on, to Jesus Christ and then through Christ to us. When a human being repents of his sin and accepts Jesus Christ as his Lord and Savior, everything God promised Abraham is passed on to us.

Birth of Esau and Jacob

In Genesis 25:24–20, we see the birth of Esau and Jacob.

And Isaac loved Esau because he did eat of his venison: but Rebekah loved Jacob.

In Genesis 25:19–34

In verse 23, it states,

> **And the Lord said unto her, two nations are in thy womb, and two manner of people shall be separated**

from thy bowels; and the one people shall be stronger than the other people; and the elder shall serve the younger.

And we see how the elder made a tremendous mistake; he did not value the firstborn right, the firstborn blessing, the firstborn privilege, and instead became hungry for a particular red pottage of lentils; after he did eat and drink and rose up, and went his way, he lost his birthright. For one plate of food, Esau lost the greatest blessing his father, Isaac, could have ever given him. He was only concerned about feeding his belly. Isn't that like a lot of Christians today selling their birthright?

This is why Esau was never blessed by God. His priorities were wrong, and his values were wrong. He did not value his inheritance. He took God's blessing very lightly. He didn't take God's promises, God's blessings, and his covenant right seriously. He didn't realize the supernatural and the fine blessing that would come upon him had he not sold his birthright.

I hope you, the reader, will realize how many mistakes people made, how many wrong choices they made, how many priorities were out of line, and how much sin separates people from God and his blessings. We are the ones that get alienated from God—were the ones to come short of God's glory, were the ones that disobeyed ignorantly, or knowingly, or because of our own desires, the will of God, which is the word of God. One of the things that I'm doing in this book, as you, the reader, and I read up on it, is making us knowledgeable about how many mistakes people made overall, which caused them never to be blessed by God. But it is important to realize that it was never God's intention not to bless them; it has always been God's intention to bless his people.

Now please understand that the purpose of this book is to teach us to realize that God is a good God, that God wants to bless us, that God is a covenant God, that God is a warning God, that God wants fellowship and common union with his people. God made us for fellowship, God wants a daily relationship with us, and God is a good heavenly Father worthy to be loved.

In Genesis 27:12–29, we see how Jacob, the younger brother of Esau, received the firstborn right and the blessing that was intended for Esau with the help of his mother, and from verses 34 to 40, we see Esau begging his father, Isaac, to bless him, and Isaac said, **"Thy brother came in with sub ability, and have taken away thy blessing."**

And then Isaac said that Jacob would be his Lord, and Esau questioned his father and said, **"Father, have you only one blessing?"**

In Genesis 32:22–32, we see the tenacity of Jacob fighting with the angel of Jehovah.

God said to him, **"I will not let you go until you bless me,"** in verses 25–32, and Jacob's name was changed to Israel, and Israel had twelve sons, and the smallest of all was Joseph, whom they called the dreamer. God gave him various dreams, and in Genesis 37:1–36, we see Joseph being envied by his brothers because of the supernatural dream that God had given him to save the Jewish people.

Now we are trying to do the very best that we can in sharing with you what happened in the Book of Genesis as chronologically as possible, but not sharing all the stories, all the chapters, and all the events so that we may understand where all God's people ended up.

We know the beautiful story of Joseph, of how because of jealousy and the supernatural vision God gave him, he was thrown into a well and, ultimately, sold to the Ishmaelites, who took him into the Pharaoh's house as a servant. After he was falsely accused, he was thrown in jail, and in time, he revealed the Pharaoh's dream.

Now notice, from a stinking jail to being second-in-command in the Pharaoh's government.

Then Pharaoh made him second-in-command over all of Egypt, and every individual bowed before him because of the position that he had. Finally, there was a drought in the land, and he had already filled the barns, and his brothers had come to Egypt to find food because they were hungry and about to die, and that is when Joseph revealed himself to his brothers, and they were sorely afraid of what Joseph might do to them.

Now we all know the story of Joseph's love for his brothers, how he forgave them and lived to be 110 years old (Genesis 50:22), and how his entire family grew and matured and greatly multiplied themselves in the land of Egypt. And after Joseph's death, there arose an evil king over the land of Egypt who didn't know Joseph and his family and enslaved the people of God for 400 years and gave them hard tasks and hard labor to build the land of Egypt with its pyramids and glorious buildings.

Now I have not used all the stories of the book of Genesis to try to explain the love, compassion, mercy, and understanding of our heavenly Father in dealing with human beings. From what you have been able to read from the Garden of Eden to the land of Egypt, we see a loving, merciful, and unchanging God who wants to relate to his people, who wants to have fellowship with his people, who wants to bless his people, and who has given us three covenants already to prove to us that he is a trustworthy God and an eternally committed heavenly Father (Genesis 3:15, the seed of the woman; Genesis 9:9, the rainbow in the sky; and Genesis 15:18, commitment to bless Abraham and his seed after him). Now, there are three more covenants in the Old Testament, for a total of six, and one in the New Testament in Hebrews 8:8–13.

Now these stories in Genesis are designed to teach us and inspire us in God's original intent for the creation and man's mission, disobedience, fall, and curse and also for us to understand the life span of humanity on earth and how God had to reduce it from 969 years to 120 years, and ultimately, God saw the continual wickedness of human beings on earth and, in Genesis 6:1–8, had to finally destroy human beings.

God had to start humanity afresh. Through Noah's descendants, God had to replenish the earth one more time.

Now in the second book of the Bible called Exodus, there are lots of beautiful stories, the history and life of Moses and how God chose him to be the liberator of the children of Israel from the bondage of Egypt, how God had to use signs and wonders from the heavens through plagues of frogs, plagues of flies, a plague on the cattle, the plague of boils, and Moses warned of hail, and finally, the plague of hail came upon them, and Moses warned about the locusts, and finally they came, the plague of darkness, and the final plague, and finally Moses warned that the final plague would be the death of the firstborn, and Pharaoh himself passed judgment upon himself, and his firstborn died.

And Passover was instituted by God

Exodus 12:1–13

Verse 21 states that Moses said to the children of Israel to take their individual lamb and to kill it and to take the blood and put it on the doorposts of their household; this way, when the death angel passed by, it would not kill anybody inside the house.

Every story in the Bible and every sacrificed lamb was the result of a holy God wanting to relate to a sinful, fallen creature. In this story, the death angel passed by the city, and the blood on the doorposts kept the firstborn of Israel from being slaughtered, and every firstborn of the Egyptians died.

The Ten Commandments are given

Exodus 20:1–5 states,

> **And God spake all these words, saying, I am the Lord thy God, which have brought thee out of the land of Egypt, out of the house of bondage.**
>
> **Thou shall have no other gods before me. Thou shall not make unto thee any graven image, or any likeness of anything that is in the heaven above, or that is in the earth beneath, or that is in the water under the earth. Thou shall not bow down thyself to them, nor serve them: for I the Lord thy God am a jealous God, visiting the iniquity of the fathers upon the children unto the third and fourth generation of them that hate me. And showing mercy unto thousands of them that love me, keep my commandments. Thou shall not take the name of the Lord thy God in vain; for the Lord will not hold him guiltless that taketh his name in vain. Remember the Sabbath day, to keep it holy. Six**

days shalt thou labor, and do all thy work: But the seventh day is the Sabbath of the Lord thy God: in it thou shall not do any work, thou, nor thy son, nor thy daughter, thy man servant, nor thy maidservant, nor thy cattle nor thy stranger that is within thy gates: For in six days the Lord made heaven and earth, the sea, and all that is in them is, and rested the seventh day: wherefore the Lord blessed the Sabbath day, and hallowed it God. Honor thy father and thy mother: that thy days may be long upon the land the Lord thy God giveth thee. Thou shall not kill. Thou shall not commit adultery. Thou shall not steal. Thou shall not bear false witness against thy neighbor. Thou shall not covet thy neighbor's house, thou shall not covet thy neighbor's wife, nor his manservant, nor his made servant, nor his ox, nor his ass, nor anything that is in thy neighbors.

Why don't I get healed?

There is a lot of wrong teaching around the land about the generational curse and why people don't get healed. If you notice in verse 1, God said, **"I am the Lord thy God, which have brought thee out of the land of Egypt, out of the house of bondage."**

Egypt is a type of the world, a house of bondage, a type of all oppression and bondage. Notice the phrase "which have brought thee out of". The Ten Commandments were given to the obedient and, with it, all of God's blessings and God's covenant.

When we do what God says in his holy scriptures and apply them to our lives and live up to his teachings, all his blessings will overtake us. And that includes health.

When God said in verse 3, "**Thou shall not have any other gods before me,**" He was referring to anything or anyone that takes up most of your time or all of your time.

He was talking about idolaters who idolize places, people, careers, games, and even in other cultures, those who idolize statues of people and animals. You can even idolize a religion, a pope, or any man of God. You can practice any religion in this world other than worshipping the God of Abraham, Isaac, and Jacob, and that's called idolizing.

So, the consequences of idolatry to the third and fourth generation is idol worshipping, anything that's your idol, anything that's your priority, anything you bow to, anything that influences you, anything that binds you, anything that snares you. Now let's get this thing straight. Blessings to those who obey and generational curses to those who disobey and idolize.

In my community, there are preachers on the radio who say the born-again Spirit-filled Christians are under the generational curse and, therefore, they need deliverance. They go to these services, they get preaching day and night, preachers lay hands on them, casting out demons and devils, and they keep coming back frustrated, irritable, angry, and with no results.

I'm about to start teaching on the most controversial topic with more question marks in Christendom since I've been born again. And misunderstood the scriptures.

A thought of being under a generational curse

In Ezekiel 18:1–32, we see part of the solution. The sinning soul shall die.

> **The word of the Lord came unto me again, saying, what mean ye, that you use this proverb concerning the land of Israel, saying the fathers have eaten sour grapes, and the children's teeth are set on edge? As I live, sayeth the Lord God, you shall not have occasion anymore to use this proverb in Israel, Behold; all souls are mine; as the soul of the father, so also the soul of the son is mine: the soul that sinneth, it shall die. But if a man be just, and do that which is lawful and**

right. And has not eaten upon the mountains, neither has lifted up his eyes to the idols of the house of Israel, neither hath defiled his neighbor' wife, neither hath come near to a menstruous woman. And hath not oppressed any, but hath restored to the debtor his pledge, has spoiled none by violence, have given his bread to the hungry, and has covered the naked with a garment. He that hath not given forth upon a usury, neither have taken any increase, that has withdrawn his hand from iniquity, has executed true judgment between man and man. Hath walked in my statutes, and hath kept my judgments, to deal truly; he is just, he shall surely live, saith the Lord God. He beget a son that is a robber, a shredder of blood, and that doeth the like to any one of these things. And that doeth not any of those duties, but even hath eaten upon the mountains, and defiled his neighbor's wife, Hath oppress the poor and needy, hath spoiled by violence, hath not restored the pledge, and hath lifted up his eyes to the idols, hath committed abomination, Hath given forth upon usury, and hath taken increase: shall he then live? He shall not live: he hath done all these abominations; he shall surely die; his blood shall be upon him. Now, low, if he beget a son, that seeth all his father's sins which ye hath done, and considereth, and doeth not such like, That hath not eaten upon the mountains, neither hath lifted up his eyes to the idols of the house of Israel, hath not defiled his neighbor's wife, Neither hath oppressed any, hath not with-Holden the pledge, neither hath spoiled by violence, but has given his bread to the hungry, and have covered the naked with a garment, That hath taken off his hand from the poor, that hath not received a usury nor increase, hath executed my judgments, hath walked in my statutes; he shall not die for the iniquity of his father, he shall surely live.

There are seven dispensations in the scriptures in the dispensation of law, which is number 5. In this dispensation, we see that the generational curse is not true. The son will not pay for the sins of the father; neither will the father pay for the sins of the son. As you can see by reading these verses, every single soul that sins, only they are responsible for the judgment of God upon their lives. And then later on, we will see how every born-again Christian in the dispensation of grace, which is number 6, who has passed from death unto life, has been bought and paid for by the blood of Jesus Christ. Therefore, it is impossible to have been redeemed from the curse of the law and still be under a curse. If that were the case, then God lied in his word.

And we all know that God is not a liar but a God of covenant and commitment, a never-ending heavenly Father.

I order to put an end to the misconception. My prayers are that every reader of this book will not only read up to the end but also give it to their pastors, their friends or family members, and anyone they know that could be sick or under this false teaching that Christians could be under a generational curse.

In the Old Testament, which is the dispensation of law, the first thirty-nine books of the Bible were written before Jesus came into the scene. We will begin by establishing that our heavenly Father is a healer.

God's name, God is a healer

(Exodus 15:26). Jehovah God equals Rafa. His name means "the Lord your healer."

God's word is God's covenant, God's commitment.

In Psalms 107:19–20, it states,

> **Then they cried out to the Lord in their trouble; He saved them out of their distresses. He sent his word and healed them.**

One of the many ways that we can get healed is found in verse 19: **"They cried out to the Lord in their trouble, and he saved them out of their distresses."** Humility is definitely a requirement to receive a miracle from God. Crying out to the Lord in these days could be through prayer, calling on a man of God to pray for you, and going to a church and when the altar call is given, not being proud, not being arrogant, and instead going to the front and letting a man of God anoint you with oil. And the Bible says the prayer of faith shall save the sick.

There are many people who won't call a brother or a preacher or won't even go to church to get prayed for because of pride. They say to themselves, "My goodness, if they see that I'm sick, they will think that I'm in sin." Sickness is something you should not be ashamed of. It is a biological disorder, or the influence of oppression, or the torment of demonic power. Either way, you should always come to God through prayer on your knees, or to a family member who knows how to pray, or to a local preacher who believes in divine healing.

Now in verse 20, we see that he sent his word and healed them. The Bible says that faith comes by hearing and hearing the word of God. Romans 10:17 states that when you hear the word of God from a family member, or a church preaching, or a message on television, or even by reading this book, the living Logos produces faith, illumination, and understanding that it is God's will to heal. Notice also that the faith that you need in order to get healed is from listening to the Word of God.

God's word is settled in heaven

Psalm 119:89 states,

> **Forever, O lord, Thy word is settled in heaven.**

It is vitally important to understand that in the beginning was the word, and that word was with God, and the word was God (John 1:1). Before human beings ever existed, God already existed. At the beginning of time, his holy scripture had already existed. God and his holy word are equal and one. God does not go back on his word because God is a God of covenant, and we have his holy scriptures to this day to prove his eternal existence, forever in heaven and on earth.

His holy word is established and settled.

In verse 90, it states,

> **Thy faithfulness continues throughout all generations; Thou didst establish the earth, and it stands.**

Our heavenly Father is a faithful God whose faithfulness continues throughout all generations, including ours. He established this planet, and it still stands, so once again, we can depend on a holy God, his holy word, and his eternal faithfulness.

So you see, we can believe, we can stand, and we can decree his holy word and covenant upon our lives and the lives of our children. Our God is a holy God and a faithful one.

God's word is a lamp and a light

Psalm 119:105 states,

> **Thy word is a lamp to my feet, And a light to my path.**

Here we see the importance of reading and understanding the Word of Almighty God because of what it represents to every reader. "A lamp unto our feet" means that if we are illuminated with God's holy word, we will not stumble because we'll be able to see which direction we're going, and his revealed knowledge will be a light unto our path.

This is why I encourage everybody to read the Word at least thirty minutes a day and set aside time for meditation on it because without the illumination and without it being a lamp unto our feet, we will definitely stumble and fall and never know the will of God for our lives, especially in the area of divine health.

God's word gives light and understanding

Psalm 119:130 states,

> **The entrance of thy words giveth light; it giveth understanding to the simple.**

As we read up on God's holy Word, it enters into our mind through the eye gate, and it produces illumination, it produces an understanding of what God's will is for our lives, it produces assurance, and we can act upon that assurance, and whatever it says, we can apply it to our everyday lives, thereby producing the results that God intended for us to have.

The beauty of God's holy Word is that he gives understanding to the simple; you don't have to be a rocket scientist to understand God's holy and simple scriptures. What I say to everybody is that you have to understand the difference between the Old Testament and the New Testament, the dispensation of law and the dispensation of grace. The dispensation of law was mostly a book of dos and don'ts, while the dispensation of grace was the fulfillment of the dispensation of law, which is unmerited favor, the gift of God through faith in our Lord Jesus Christ so that no man would boost.

God's desire, man's choice

Proverbs 4:20–22 states,

> **My son, give attention to my words; incline your ear to my sayings. Do not let them depart from your sight; Keep them in the midst of your heart. For they are life to those who find them, And health to all their whole body. Watch over your heart with all diligence, For from it flow the springs of life.**

In Jeremiah 30:17, it states,

> **"But I will restore you to health and heal your wounds," declares the Lord.**

Psalms 103:-4 states,

> **Praise the Lord, O my soul, and forget not all his benefits-who forgives all your sins and heals all your diseases, who redeems your life from the pit and crowns you with love and compassion.**

Exodus 23:25 states,

> **But you shall serve the Lord your God, and he will bless your bread and your water. And I will take sickness away from the midst of you.**

This is very simple to understand. God wants us to pay attention to his words, not to your feelings, not to your mistakes, not to your shortcomings, not to people's views and ways of your life. We are to pay attention to the words of Almighty God through his Word. We are to read it for ourselves, to incline our ear to his sayings. When people have a problem, they are prone to look for the solution elsewhere from God's holy Word. I have not found a need, a problem, or a situation that I've not been able to find an answer for in God's holy Word.

God is encouraging us to look to his holy Word for answers in every area of our lives, which is our spirit, our soul, and our body. He also has the solution for the necessary concentration of our minds, His blessings upon our legal life, and His blessings upon our relational lives. In essence, His precious Word has the solution for everything we will ever need for the rest of our lives on this earth.

God does not want us to let His word depart from our lives; He wants His views, His ways, and His values to take center stage in our thought life, in our speech, and in our behavior and for us to hide those principles in our hearts.

Notice what He says in verse 22, **"For they are life to them that find them, and health to all their whole body."**

Isn't this really smart? If we apply His views, if we apply these values, if we apply His word, which is His value system, He says we would have found life and health in every part of our physical body. You know, it's amazing. As I write this book, faith is rising up within me and making me stronger and bolder as I speak into this microphone, and I see these words being printed on my computer.

Everything that goes through my eyes as I read the holy Word of God goes into my mind, and through meditation, I bring it into my heart, and it strengthens the hidden man of my heart, for from it flows the springs of life. This is truly amazing and supernatural.

So many people are sick in the world, not knowing that as they read the Word of God for themselves and allow these holy anointed scriptures to penetrate their souls and ultimately go into their hearts, they can get totally healed by just reading. Of course, we will look into why some of them are not healed, which is the nature of this book.

Now from now on, this is where it gets really exciting because I will bring this teaching closer to home and to our individual needs as human beings.

What is healing? It's a change of health with divine help

We're going to explore the new dispensation of grace, the dispensation of the outpouring of the Holy Spirit, and the dispensation of God's ultimate and final blessing upon humanity through the death, burial, and resurrection of our Lord and Savior Jesus Christ and his sacrificial substitution on the cross.

The first thing we want to understand is the three-time zones written in the Bible: the past, the present, and the future.

It is vitally important to understand that we are living in the future from a godly Biblical standpoint. When the Bible says, "In the beginning," that is the past, before any human beings, before the Word of God, the written Bible. Before anything ever existed, God, Jesus Christ, the Holy Spirit, and obviously his word had already existed.

The entire Old Testament was always predicting what would happen when the Messiah would step into the human race, and as you very well know, Jesus Christ of Nazareth fulfilled all nine hundred prophecies about him in the Old Testament by becoming God the Son, Emmanuelle, God with us, and he went about teaching, preaching, and healing all that were oppressed of the devil, for God was with him.

The Old Testament was the past, the New Testament is still in the past, and we who are in the future from a Bible perspective, when we read the New Testament, we are reading about something that took place in the past, something that was accomplished on our behalf on the cross, something that took place on our behalf, someone who substituted the human race and took upon himself the guilt, condemnation, sin, damnation, and curse, having canceled out the certificate of debt consisting of decrees against us and that was hostile to us, and he has taken it out of the way, having nailed it to the cross (Colossians 2:14).

Now let's see what the Word of God says in the 3 epistle of John verse 2:

> **Beloved, I wish above all things, that thou mayest prosper and be in health, even as thy soul prospereth.**

This teaching is approximately ninety years in the future from Jesus's time.

There are three kinds of prosperity that the Word of God teaches us that we should have in abundance. The first one is that our soul prospers. Our soul has three functions: Number 1, knowledge—that part of our brain is the subconscious, where we store all the information that we acquire through our lives through education and good or bad experiences. Number 2, choice—the power to choose, the power to decide. We're made a free moral agents with the capacity to choose; we are not robots. Number 3, emotions—we have an eternal soul with knowledge, free will, and emotions. Our emotions are not good or bad; they are there for us to release stress, cry out to God, and be humbled.

But emotions are not to be trusted. One day we are emotionally high, then another day, we're emotionally low.

As our soul prospers with the knowledge of God's holy word, then we will make our way prosperous and be in good health.

The word "prosper" means to have everything we need in the material realm, like a career, a job, or a ministry, so that we can produce finances and be able to obtain prosperity and be lacking in nothing.

But the teaching today in this book is about being in good health, that our mind would be thinking accurately and that our bodies, every member thereof, including the heart, our lungs, our kidneys, our stomach, our cardiovascular system, and many more parts in our bodies that I am not mentioning, be completely whole and healthy.

Now we certainly know exactly what is the will of God for our whole being, our spirit, our soul, and our body. Now let's go back to 2,725 years. We are now living in 2013, and the prophet Isaiah prophesied approximately 712 years before Jesus's time, totaling 2,725 years.

Isaiah 53:3–6 states,

> **He was despised and forsaken of men, A man of sorrows, and acquainted with grief; And like one from whom men hide their face, and we did not esteem him. Surely our grief's he himself bore, and our sorrows he carried; Yet we ourselves esteemed him stricken, smitten of God, and afflicted. But he was pierced through for our transgressions, He was crushed for our iniquities; The chastening for our well-being, fell upon him, And by his stripes we are healed. All of us like sheep have gone astray; But the Lord has caused the iniquities of us all to fall upon him.**

"Pierced through" means holes being made in his body for our transgressions; every wrong thing, every stupid mistake, every wrong choice, and every act of immoral behavior is considered a transgression.

There were holes being made in his body. He took upon himself our punishment. What we deserved, he took it upon himself. (I just saw the movie *The Passion of the Christ*. He was beaten so badly, had so many holes in his body, that as I watched that, tears were coming down my cheeks.) Can you really understand the substitution here? Please understand this happened 2,013 years ago but was prophesied 712 years prior to that.

He was crushed for our iniquities. What is iniquity? Deviation from what is right, wickedness, gross injustice, wrongful act, unjust thing or deed, abomination, injustice, sin. Can you see him taking our place on the cross? In verse 6, the Lord has caused the iniquities of us all to fall upon him.

He was beaten, spat upon, mistreated, and chastened for our well-being, which fell upon him, and by his stripes, we are healed. Notice the present tense.

Notice here his substitutional role on the cross, taking our place, receiving the punishment for our sins, receiving the stripes for our healing, and being chastised for our iniquities. Remember, this was prophesied even before Jesus came into the scene and died in our place. The judgment of God that came upon humanity was placed upon him so that we could be free so that we can be sound, and so that we could be physically whole. (When is he going to do this?)

This is one of the prophecies that Jesus fulfilled when he walked out of the portals of glory to step into the natural and fulfill his role as the sacrificed Lamb that takes away the sin of the world.

This is what Jesus Christ of Nazareth did. For us to receive health, he was willing to die in our place; to redeem us from the strongholds of Satan and the legal right he had upon us, Jesus Christ of Nazareth came to destroy the works of the devil, and he did.

We will look back only 2,013 years from today on Matthew 8:17 to see Jesus walking on earth and fulfilling the prophecies of the prophet Isaiah, and it reads,

In order that what was spoken through Isaiah the prophet might be fulfilled, saying, "**He Himself Took Our Infirmities, and Carried Away Our Diseases.**"

Jesus fulfilled this chapter and verse in his biblical present time. Our time started with Jesus's birth, and that is why it is considered present, and we are in the future.

In this verse, Jesus Christ of Nazareth is fulfilling Isaiah's prophecies 712 years prior to his coming, and the verse itself explains it all. He himself took our infirmities. Notice this explanation that says, "He himself took." When this fulfillment took place, it was at the present time. He was fulfilling the past prophecies in the present. Always remember that the New Testament 2,013 years ago was the present fulfillment of the Old Testament. We are in the future from a biblical standpoint, and when we look back and understand what Jesus did in our place, we must understand that in our new covenant through the blood of the Lord Jesus Christ, one of our biblical rights is total deliverance and total well-being in our spirit, soul, and body.

Therefore, we have no right to be sick or to let the enemy put infirmities upon us because Jesus Christ of Nazareth took them from us. Not only did he take our infirmities from us, but he also carried away our diseases. Can you see why the enemy has been trespassing on God's property illegally? The enemy can knock on your door, but you don't have to let him in by neglect or by negative confession of whose infirmity is upon you. Or because of a lack of knowledge.

People say, "I have a cold." And I say give it back. The cold is not ours. If it was ours, Jesus could not have taken it away or carried it away. Can you see it? Traditionally, we have always personalized sickness, disease, and infirmities as if they were ours. They may be in our bodies because they have trespassed illegally, but they are not ours.

Now there are sicknesses that are the by-product of malnutrition; that is a totally different story, and we will address that later on.

You hear people say, "I am getting sick," and I say to them, "Don't get it." You hear people say, "I'm catching a cold," and I say to them, "Don't, don't catch it, let it go by." You hear people say, "I can't do this" or "I can't do that," explaining away why the infirmity that the enemy has put upon them should be on them, and I say to them, "If Jesus took your infirmities and he carried away your diseases, why do you want to get them back?" Negative confession, we will pick up on this a little further down in the teaching.

In the next teachings, we will look in the future from Jesus's death, burial, and resurrection approximately seventy years in the future, where the apostle Peter wrote in Peter 2:24 (American Standard),

And he himself bore our sins in his body on the cross, that we might die to sin and live to righteousness; for by his stripes you were healed.

In this verse, the first thing I want you to understand is that Peter is writing about what Jesus Christ himself did on the cross some seventy years back in time. Once again, I want to bring to your attention that the prophecies of Isaiah were the past, the gospel of Matthew was the present, and the epistle of Peter was the future. And we are 2,013 years in the future.

The second thing I want you to see in this verse is the quote, "That we might die to sin, and live to righteousness." In other words, progressively in our communion with God, we would live in the right standing with him, fault less, and with other people, treating other people righteously; that is what it means when he says, "Live to righteousness."

Verse 24 states, **"For by his stripes you were healed."** In this verse, we see a prerequisite in order to claim that we were healed, and it has to do with our conduct in relation to God and other people. A lot of times, we cannot say that because our minds are clouded with negative influence and our way of life is below every Christian standard.

Now here we have seen the three time zones: the first is 712 years before Jesus, the second is the present ministry of Jesus, and the third is Peter's teaching 70 years in the future.

Examples of Jesus delivering and healing the afflicted

Matthew 9:12 states,

> **When Jesus heard that, he said to them, "those who were well have no need of a physician, but those who are sick.**

In these examples, we will see Jesus Christ of Nazareth himself performing all kinds of miracles. They are there so that we will understand God's desire for our total well-being.

Matthew 9:27–31 states,

> **And as Jesus passed on from there, two blind men followed him, crying out and saying, "Have mercy on us, Son of David!" And after he had come into the house, the blind men came up to him, and Jesus said to them, "To you believe that I am able to do this?" They said to him, "Yes, Lord." Then he touched their eyes, saying, "Be it done to you according to your faith". And then their eyes were opened. And Jesus sternly warned them, saying, "See here; let no one know about this!" But they went out and spread the news about him in all that land.**

There are some things that we need to see clearly in these passages. Two blind men followed him. When we are sick, we need to follow the instructions of Jesus. The word "crying out" means we need to do anything that needs to be done in order to get the Lord Jesus's attention.

In this particular instance, Jesus asked the men, "Do you believe that I'm able to do this?" And they said, "Yes, Lord." In order to receive a miracle from God, we must believe that he is able to do it. The moment they said, "Yes, Lord," in total submission to his authority, then he touched their eyes and said, "Be it done to you according to your faith." In Hebrews 11:6, it says, **"For without faith it is impossible to please him, for he who comes to God must believe that he is, and that he is a rewarder of those who seek him."**

These two men were seeking a miracle from God through Jesus Christ, and they got it.

We must all look at the prerequisite in order to receive a miracle. Please look carefully at the underlined words because they are the clue to receiving your inheritance.

A new scenario with a different requirement

In Matthew 8:5–13, it states,

> **And when he had entered Capernaum, a centurion and came to him, entreating Him, and saying, "Lord, my servant is lying paralyzed at home, suffering great pain." And he said to him, "I will come and heal him." But the centurion answered and said, "Lord, I am not worthy for you to come under my roof, but just say the word and my servant will be healed. "For I, too, am a man under authority, with soldiers under me; and I say to this one, 'go!' and he goes, and to another, 'come!' and he comes, and to my slave, 'Do this!' and he doeth it." Now when Jesus heard this, He marveled, and said to those who were following, "Truly I say to you, I have not found such great faith with anyone in Israel. "And I say to you, that many shall come East and West, and recline at the table with Abraham, and Isaac, and Jacob in the kingdom of heaven; But the sons of the kingdom shall be cast out into outer darkness; in that place there shall be weeping and gnashing of teeth." And Jesus said to this centurion, "Go your way; let it be done to you as you have believed." And the servant was healed that very hour.**

(1) The centurion called him Lord. (2) He explained his case. (3) He knew that Jesus would heal his servant. (4) He understood Jesus's authority over sickness, disease, and infirmity. (5) He understood his authority over demon power. (6) He understood the power of Jesus's word and how the elements would obey him, the wind, the waves, the multiplication power, and his word.

The centurion knew Jesus's authority over everything, and he said, "Just say the word, and my servant will be healed." My god, we have four gospels full of Jesus's word, and a lot of people do not believe it. This divine revelation is what everybody needs to receive a miracle from God himself.

The word of God is God. Jesus is God the Son manifested in the word and becoming flesh. In John 1:1, it reads,

> **In the beginning was the word, and the word was with God, and the word was God, and the Word became flesh, and dwelt among us, and we beheld his glory, glory as of the only begotten from the father, full of grace and truth.**

When we hold the Word of God in our hands, his holy scriptures, we are holding that love letter that became flesh, and that is Jesus Christ, the only begotten of the Father, full of grace and truth. And like the centurion who said, "Just say the word," we have an entire Bible full of his words; therefore, we should believe everything the Word says about Jesus Christ and his divine authority.

Some sickness could be the result of sin

Mark 2:1–12 states,

> **And many were gathered together, so that there was no longer room, even near the door; and he was speaking the word to them. And they came, bringing to him a paralytic, carried by four men. And being unable to get to him because of the crowd, they removed the roof above him; and when they had dug an opening, they let down the pallet on which the paralytic was lying. And Jesus seeing their faith said to the paralytic, "My son, your sins are forgiven."**

Which is easier, to say to the paralytic, "Your sins are forgiven"; or to say, "Arise, and take up your pallet and walk"? "But in order that you may know that the Son of Man has authority on earth to forgive sins." He said to the paralytic, "I say to you, rise, take up your pallet and go home." And he rose and immediately took up the pallet I went out in the sight of all; so that they were all amazed and were glorifying God, saying, "We have never seen anything like this."

Now we don't know for sure what kind of sin he had committed, and as a result, he was sick from his disobedience to the law of Moses, but in this particular case, we see Jesus Christ forgiving his sins and telling him to pick up his pallet and walk. Whatever the case might have been, this book you are reading is about self-examination, doing away with excuses, doing away with ignorance, and moving forward to receiving the best that God has for our lives. It is not about judging someone's life, but it's about finding the root cause of the problem as to "Why don't I get healed?"

Why haven't I received healing? You have seen three different scenarios where Jesus himself has dealt totally differently with every one of the people that had come to him. First, he dealt with the two blind men, asking them if they would believe what he was able to do, and they said, "Yes, Lord, we believe." The second person he dealt with was the centurion, and he said to Jesus, "Just say the word and I will believe." The third person he dealt with did not need any faith; all he needed was to find forgiveness for his sins from the violation of the law of Moses. These are three perfectly different scenarios so that we may examine ourselves in light of our communion with Christ.

Mark 5:22–24 states,

> **And one of the synagogue officials named Gairus came up, and upon seeing him, Fell at his feet, and entreated him earnestly, say, "My little daughter is at the point of death; please come and lay your hands on her, that she may get well and live." And he went off with him; and a great multitude was following him and pressing in on him.**

Now from verse 25 to verse 34, there is a different story there about a woman with an issue of blood, and I will get to that story after I finish this one.

Verses 35–43 states,

> **While he was still speaking, they came from the house of the synagogue official, saying, "Your daughter has died; Why trouble the teacher anymore?" But Jesus, overhearing what was being spoken, said to the synagogue official, "do not be afraid any longer, only believe." And he allowed no one to follow with him, except Peter and James and John the brother of James. And they came to the house of the synagogue official; and he beheld a commotion, and people loudly weeping and wailing. And entering in, He said to them, "Why make a commotion and weep? The child has not died, but is sleep." And they began laughing at him. But putting them all out, He took along the child's father and mother and his own companions, and entered the room where the child was. And taking the child by the hand, He said to her, "Talithakum!" (Which translated means, "Little girl, I say to you, arise!") And immediately the girl rose and began to walk; for she was 12 years old. And immediately they were completely astounded. And he gave them strict orders that no one should know about this; and he said that something should be given her to eat.**

Even in impossible situations, God Almighty, through Jesus Christ, can perform a miracle despite unbelief, but one thing is certain in this passage, Jesus had to remove the doubters. Miracles, signs and wonders, divine healing, and divine health require you to surround yourself with people that believe because unbelievers short-circuit the power of God, and when a man of God anointed with the Holy Spirit is praying, there has to be an expectancy of faith in the atmosphere for signs and wonders to occur.

What strikes me the most in this passage is that despite the fact that the child had already died and did not want him to trouble Jesus any longer, this might not have even been a Christian, a follower of Jesus, or even a believer in his signs and wonders. He was only unofficial of the synagogue, and who knows what he believed, but he said the magic word, "Please come and lay your hands on her that she may get well and live." He believed that Jesus could do the work even after the child had already died.

When our situation, when our challenge, when our scenario seems dark and even almost impossible, that's when our heavenly Father comes to the rescue, and that is where the supernatural touches the natural. Never give up. Just close your eyes, lift both of your arms to the sky, and say, "Abba, Father, I've come to the end of my rope, and I need a supernatural touch."

Then name your situation, whatever it may be, regardless of how tough it may look. Our heavenly Father lives, and in Jesus's name, he will listen to our prayers. Even as I speak into this microphone, I know that he lives because I sense him in my office even as I speak.

Our heavenly Father is a good God. He loves us, and he will never leave us nor forsake us. He promised that in his holy and eternal scriptures, the Bible.

We must be like Jacob. Hold on to God and his promises until we see a breakthrough.

Now in between that story we just finished from verse 25 to verse 34, there was a different scenario that required pressing through regardless of the opposition.

In Mark 5:25–34, we see the next scenario that took place:

> **And a woman who had had hemorrhage for 12 years, and had endured much at the hands of many physicians, and had spent all that she had and was not helped at all, but rather had grown worse, after hearing about Jesus, came up in the crowd behind**

> **him, and touched his cloak. For she thought, "If I just touched his garment, I shall get well." And immediately the flow of blood was dried up; and she felt in her body that she was healed of her affliction. And immediately Jesus, perceiving in himself that the power proceeding from him had gone forth, turned around in the crowd and said, "Who touched my garments?" And his disciples said to him, "You see the multitude pressing in on you, and you say 'Who touched me?'" And he looked around to see the woman who had done this. But the woman fearing and trembling, aware of what had happened to her, came and fell down before him, and told him the whole truth. And he said to her, "Daughter your faith has made you well; go in peace, and be healed of your affliction."**

When I read this story, it brought back memories of my own mother, who had a hemorrhage, and back then, all they could do was chemotherapy in order to treat her affliction. I was only fifteen years of age and did not know Jesus, the healer, and after two years of chemotherapy, they gave her up to die. In a total of four years later, she died.

In verse 34, Jesus said to the woman, "Daughter, your faith has made you well, go in peace, and be healed of your affliction." As I say these words, tears are coming down my cheeks. Had I been born again, had I known then what I know today, perhaps my mother would have been alive. Certainly, I would have prayed for her and shared with her the substitutional role of Jesus on the cross so that we could be made whole. Why is it so tough to believe the truth of his mission on this earth on our behalf? It is easier to believe a lie. My heart's desire is that when you finish reading this book, the entrance of God's word into your spirit will give you the necessary knowledge for you to inherit your inheritance, which is wellness in your spirit, soul, and body, and is free. It's what Jesus bought and paid for us.

In Mark 8:22–26 is a very interesting scenario:

> **And they came to Bethsaida. And they brought a blind man to him, and entreated him to touch him. And taking the blind man by the hand, He brought him out of the village; and after spitting on his eyes, and laying his hands upon him, He asked him, "Do you see anything?" And he looked up and said, "I see men, for I am seeing them like trees, walking about." Then again he laid his hands upon his eyes; and he looked intently and was restored, and began to see everything clearly. And he sent him to his home, saying, "Do not even enter the village."**

How would you like to be in a church service and have the preacher call you up front, look you straight in the eyes, and spit in your eyes? That is rather odd, isn't it?

This is a very interesting scenario. It is very important that we realize who it is that is praying for us. Once you have established that it is a reputable man of God, then you can allow him to lay hands on you, anoint you with oil, and do the prayer of faith, and the Bible says we shall recover.

In these new modern days, there are some things that we can let the preacher do to us, like telling us to run around the congregation, putting his hand on our head forcefully, telling us to get on our knees, telling us to go on a two- or three-day fast, and telling us to go to a Bible study that teaches the Word of God and divine healing.

It is important to understand that the real child of God, bought and paid for by the blood of Jesus Christ, filled with the Holy Spirit, with the evidence of speaking in other tongues, cannot be demon possessed or be under any curse. He can only be influenced or under the oppression of tormenting demons, influenced by a spirit of disobedience, deceived by tormenting demons, but not demon-possessed. Please know the difference between "influence," "oppression," "tormenting," "a clouded mind," "stress," "discouragement," "rejected," and "depressed." Now all the symptoms come from the outside as fiery darts of the enemy and not necessarily from the inside of human beings, thereby causing us to be sick. That is why the preacher has to bind the devil, cast out his influence, and command the devil to leave the human body in Jesus's name.

Also, never let anybody do deliverance on you, lay hands on your belly, and command the devil to come out if you are saved and filled by the Holy Spirit, and also to bind any generational curse on your life because we have already been bought and paid for by the blood of Jesus Christ and from the legal right the devil had over our lives. And we do not belong to ourselves; we are God's property, and the enemy may be trespassing on it.

Now we can let the preacher ask God to do recreative miracles to heal a particular member of our body, but be very careful with those who want to do deliverance on you. They may be doing more harm than good by not even knowing it.

Why permit sickness?

The answer is found in John 9:1–7:

> **And he passed by, He saw a man blind from birth. And his disciples asked him, saying, "Rabbi, who sinned, this man or his parents, that he should be born blind?" Jesus answered, "It was neither that this man sinned, nor his parents; but it was in order that the works of God might be displayed in him. "We must work the works of him who sent me, as long as it is day; night is coming, when no man can work. "While I am in the world, I am the light of the world." When he had said these, He spat on the ground, and made clay of the spittle, and applied the clay to his eyes, and said unto him, "Go, washed in the pool of Siloam" [which is translated as Sent]. And so he went away and washed and came back seeing.**

In this passage, we once again destroy the philosophy of a generational curse, which we have already addressed in Ezekiel 18:1–20. The most important part that we can get out of this particular scenario is that neither the parents nor the person sinned but that the works of God might be displayed in him. The person doing the praying and the person receiving that prayer must be in one accord for deliverance or for the miracle of God to take place.

I have seen a lot of people whose child is bedridden with paralysis, some biological disorder, or some birth defect that had absolutely nothing to do with the parents or a generational curse. I've even seen preachers' kids sick with incurable diseases or with retardation in mind, and a lot of them have been under a tremendous amount of rejection and condemnation. And they have even tried to pray for them with no results because they are too emotionally bound to them, too close to their children, and have also been lied to.

God is not willing that anybody should perish but that everybody should come to repentance and be healed from the crown of their heads to the soles of their feet. God wants you whole, in your spirit, in your mind, and in your body. We must not let the enemy lie to us any longer. Whoever the Son of God sets free is free in deed.

In Luke 7:11–19, it states,

> **And it came about soon afterwards, that he went to a city called Nain; and his disciples were going along with him, accompanied by a large multitude. Now as he approached the gate of the city, behold, a dead man was being carried out, the only son of his mother, and she was a widow; and a sizeable crowd from the city was with her. And when the Lord saw her, He felt compassion for her, and said to her, "Do not weep." And he came up and touched the coffin; and the bearers came to a halt. And he said, "Young man, I say to you, arise!" And the dead man sat up, and he began to speak. And Jesus gave him back to his mother. And fear gripped them all, and**

> **they began glorifying God, saying, "A great prophet has arisen among us!" And, "God has visited his people!"**

Now in these seven examples of Jesus Christ of Nazareth's desire to heal us, do you have any doubt in your mind at all of God's desire, Jesus's desire, and the Holy Spirit's desire to set us free from bondage, from all oppression, sicknesses, diseases, and infirmities? Should we have any questions at all?

When Jesus Christ of Nazareth comes inside the human heart, we're made brand-new, we have a new birth, and we are a new creation (2 Corinthians 5:17). Then comes the second manifestation of grace, which is the baptism in the Holy Spirit, and with that baptism comes the fruit of the Spirit in 1 Corinthians 13:1–13 and the gifts of the Spirit found in 1 Corinthians 12:7–11.

Jesus Christ of Nazareth did not keep the supernatural power inside himself. When he comes inside us in the person of the Holy Spirit, he brings gifts. Let us examine them now.

In order to be prayed for and have these fiery darts cast away from us, if a man of God before us is filled with the Holy Spirit, he has nine gifts inside him.

In 1 Corinthians 12:7–11, it states,

> **But to each one is given the manifestation of the spirit for the common good. Four to one is given the word of wisdom through the spirit, to another the word of knowledge according to the same spirit; To another faith by the same spirit, and to another gifts of healing by the one spirit. and to another the affecting of miracles, and to another prophecy, and to another discerning of spirits, to another various kinds of tongues, and to another the interpretation of tongues. But one and the same Spirit works all these things, distributing to each one individually just as he wills.**

The manifestation of the Holy Spirit is for the common good. Anybody filled with the Holy Spirit will not do wrong consciously. He could do wrong ignorantly but not willingly. The baptism in the Holy Spirit is so that we may manifest the gifts with supernatural power over the oppression of the enemy and his tormenting demon power attacking human beings and putting all kinds of diseases and infirmities on their bodies.

As you can see, there are nine gifts: three that reveal something, three that know something, and three that do something. When you see verse 9, we underline gifts of healing. Jesus Christ of Nazareth comes in the third person of the divine Trinity. He saves us, and he seals us, then comes the baptism in the Holy Spirit, which brings the gifts of the Holy Spirit inside the human body, thereby giving us the authority and the power to tread over serpents and scorpions and over all the power of the enemy (Luke 10:19), thereby empowering us to lay hands on the sick, and they shall recover.

Remember, the gifts of the Holy Spirit are given by God himself as he wills to every individual that receives the baptism. If you are a Christian and you have received the baptism in the Holy Spirit, and the enemy has put infirmities or diseases on your body, remember the supernatural power that is in your belly. You can lay your hands on yourself. You can put your hands on your forehead. You can put your hand on your subconscious. You can put your hands on your lower back, on your chest, and on your throat. You can anoint yourself with oil and cast away that influence that has jumped upon you and command it to leave in Jesus's name. More about your God-given rights further along.

Examples of healing done through Peter and Paul

In Acts 5:14–16, we see examples of healing done through Peter and Paul:

> **And all the more believers in the Lord, multitudes of men and women, were constantly added to their number; to such an extent that they even carried**

the sick out into the streets, and laid them on cots and pallets, so that when Peter came by, at least his shadow my fall on any one of them. And also the people from the cities in the vicinity of Jerusalem were coming together, bringing people who were sick or afflicted with unclean spirits; and they were all being healed.

In this scenario, the apostle Peter, even after he denied Jesus three times, after he received the baptism in the Holy Spirit, received the power (Acts 1:8). The anointing of God was so strong that they even brought the sick and laid them on the floor so that the shadow of Peter, when he passed by, would fall upon the sick, and they were being healed.

Every Christian, every Spirit-filled Christian baptized in the Holy Spirit, with the evidence of speaking in other tongues, has at least three or four gifts of the Holy Spirit operating in their lives. We need to evaluate which of these gifts are operating in our lives so that we may tap into the supernatural. Now remember, God is a spirit, God became flesh in the person of Jesus Christ, and Jesus Christ in the person of the Holy Spirit, who came inside us, bringing to us the gifts that we already mentioned in 1 Corinthians 12:7–11. Therefore, every Christian can exercise the power of Almighty God through prayer. God is no respecter of persons.

This is very powerful. Look at Acts 2:38–41:

And Peter said to them, "Repent, and let each of you be baptized in the name of Jesus Christ for the forgiveness of your sins; and you shall receive the gift of the Holy Spirit. "For the promise is for you and your children, and for all who are far off, as many as the Lord our God shall call to himself." And with many other words he solemnly testified and kept on exhorting them, saying "Be saved from this perverse generation!" So then, those who had received his

> **word were baptized; and there were added that day about three thousand souls.**

My prayer is that everybody reading this book may tap into this miracle. When we repent and receive Jesus Christ as our Lord and Savior and are baptized in water, we are then ready to receive the baptism in the Holy Spirit, with the fruits and the gifts, because that promise in verse 39 was for them, and it is for us, and it is for our children even as many as the Lord shall call to himself. If you are saved, if we are saved, then we are called by God, so this particular gift, which is the baptism in the Holy Spirit with these manifestations, is for everyone. This is what really turned me on to Christianity—forgiveness of sin, cleansed from all unrighteousness, made the righteousness of God in Christ, baptized in the Holy Spirit, the same Holy Spirit the apostles received. So these signs shall follow them that believe. I believe. Do you believe it? More on this power later.

In Acts 9:11–12, it states,

> **And God was performing extraordinary miracles by the hands of Paul, so that handkerchiefs or aprons were even carried from his body to the sick, and the diseases left them and the evil spirits went out.**

Notice here that evil spirits were coming out of them through handkerchiefs or aprons. The anointing of the Holy Spirit saturated these articles, and signs and wonders were being done by God through them. Lots of people justify their powerlessness because when they pray, a lot of things don't happen.

In the next few verses, we will see that this supernatural power through the baptism of the Holy Spirit is for all of us also, not just for the apostles of old. Jesus Christ is the same yesterday, today, and forever. If people were baptized in the Holy Spirit, then they are baptized in the Holy Spirit today, and we must believe that because God said it in Acts 2:39.

God is not a liar. His Word doesn't lie, and we can believe every word and act upon them, and we will see signs and wonders. I have prayed for blind people, and they can see. I have prayed for people in coma, and they have come to life. I have prayed for dying people, and God has extended them fifteen extra years. I have prayed for people with HIV, and they have been delivered and set free. I have prayed for people's eyes and for God to do a creative miracle, and they received their miracle. I have prayed for people with cancer, and they have been healed. I could tell you a lot more testimonies, but let's continue on with the book.

God-given authority

Now let's look at our God-given authority as born-again believers.

Let's look at John 14:11–17:

> **Believe me that I am in the father, and the father in me; otherwise believe on account of the works themselves. Truly, truly, I say to you, he who believes in me, the works that I do shall he do also; and greater works than these shall he do; because I go to the father. And whatsoever you ask in my name, that will I do, that the father may be glorified in the son. If you ask me anything in my name, I will do it. If you love me, you will keep my commandments. And I will ask the father, and he will give you another helper, that he may be with you forever; that is the spirit of truth, whom the world cannot receive, because it does not behold him or know him, but you know him because he abides with you, and will be with you.**

Let's look at these words carefully. This is Jesus Christ talking. In verse 11, it says, "Believe me that I am in the father, and the father is in me, otherwise believe me on account of the works themselves." These are powerful words from God Almighty through Jesus Christ himself. If we cannot believe these words, then the entire book is a lie. Every child of God, every born-again believer who has received Jesus Christ as his Lord and Savior, can do these works because he said he will ask the Father to give us another helper, comforter, the third person of the divine Trinity, who is the one that will be doing all these signs and wonders through us.

Let's look at John 15:7–16:

> **If you abide in me, and my words abide in you, ask whatever you wish, and it shall be done for you.**

With this particular verse, I have actually prayed so that it won't rain, and it hasn't rained. When Jesus said, "If you abide in me," that means to abide in his word as a disciple, and "my words abide in you," that means you make his word a part of your daily walk. You shall ask anything, anything we desire, anything we want, and it shall be done for us.

God is a holy, righteous, and true heavenly Father. When Jesus Christ talks, it is God talking through him. When the God-man speaks, we can take his word literally, believe it, and act upon it. God cannot and would not lie to us.

You did not choose me, but I chose you, and appointed you, that you should go and bear fruit, and that your fruit should remain, that whatever you ask the father in my name, He may give to you.

This is wonderful. This is glorious. If you are reading this book and you have passed from death unto life, and you have a personal relationship with Christ through your born-again experience, you have been a chosen vessel of God to manifest the supernatural power of the precious Holy Spirit with his gifts through you in the laying of your hands on the sick, and they will recover.

I don't know what these verses are doing to you as you read this book, but as I dictate them, someone is rising up within me and making me strong and bold. The precious Holy Spirit is welling up within me out of my belly as a river of living waters. He is the third person of the divine Trinity, and God is a spirit, and they who worship him must worship him in spirit and in truth.

In Luke 10:19, it states,

> **Behold, I have given you authority to tread upon serpents and scorpions, and over all the power of the enemy, and nothing shall injure you.**

Serpents and scorpions and all the power of the enemy have to do with Satan, the devil, his demons, and all principalities and powers and rulers of this dark age and spiritual wickedness in high places.

Every believer, every child of Almighty God, has been delegated, charged, and empowered by God Himself through the power of the Holy Spirit to tread over serpents and scorpions and over all the power of the enemy. This is you and me, and nothing will hurt us or injure us.

If we only knew the supernatural power, the creative power, of the third person of the Holy Trinity that lives within us, (a) we would not be defeated, (b) our minds would not be clouded, and (c) we would not accept sickness, disease, and infirmity to be put upon us. We have to develop a "Christ in me" mentality and not a "sin in me" mentality.

Our spirit man has to control our mind, control our body, and control our entire being. The Bible says that the lust of the eyes, the lust of the flesh, and the pride of life are our greatest enemies (1 John 2:16). No child of God has any business being enslaved by the enemy, enslaved by the desires of his eyes, enslaved by the desires of his flesh, and enslaved by the pride of life—these are our greatest enemies. If you have truly made a commitment to follow Jesus, to be a disciple, to be a doer of his word on the authority of his holy scriptures, you have to be free, for whoever the Son of God sets free is free indeed.

Jesus Christ came to set us free and to deliver us from the power of the enemy. Always remember, he came to destroy the works of the devil, and he did.

The enemy has always tried to hinder us, put sickness, disease, and infirmities in our bodies, and put roadblocks, sidetracks, and obstacles to keep us from doing the will of God. The New Testament is the will of Almighty God, the fulfillment of the entire will of God for our lives. The Old Testament was a foreshadowing of what was going to happen. The New Testament is the fulfillment of a better covenant with better promises through the sacrificed Lamb that took away the sin of the world and bought eternal redemption for human beings through his precious blood.

Everything we will ever need is found in God's constitution, his will, which is the same thing as his testament, which is our inheritance.

He substituted us, he paid for us with his blood, he generated our spirit, he delivered us from the devil, he set us free, he removed us from the kingdom of the devil and translated us to the kingdom of his dear Son (Colossians 1:13–14), then he put the third person of the divine Trinity within us. We became his temple on earth, then he gave us authority and power over all the power of the enemy, and then he commissioned us to go around the world and preach his holy good news, the gospel, his unmerited favor toward those who believe. To God be the glory. Great things he has done. Everything we have read has already taken place by just being born again.

Then he gives us his supernatural power, his delegated authority, and commissions us.

This commission has been given and ordered by God.

In Mark 16:15–18, it states,

> **And he said to them "Go into all the world and preach the gospel to all creation. He who has believed and has been baptized shall be saved; but he who has disbelieved shall be condemned. And these signs will accompany those who have believed: in my name they will cast out demons, they will speak with new tongues; they will pick up serpents, and if they drink any deadly poison, it shall not hurt them; they will lay hands on the sick, and they will recover."**

A) must believe, B) must be baptized, C) will be saved, D) and that these signs will accompany those who believe, that's you and me, E) in his name we will cast out demons, F) if we drink any deadly poison it will not hurt us, F) And we shall lay hands on the sick, and they will recover.

What must I do to get healed?

Then what must I do to get healed? The answer is found in Matthew 13:15:

> **For the heart of this people has become dull, And with their ears they scarcely hear, And they have closed their eyes Lest they should see with their eyes, And hear with their ears, And understand with their hearts and return, And I should healed them.**

Question number 1, check your heart. Are you following Jesus because of what you can get out of him or because you are grateful for what he has done for you on the cross?

Number 2, do you listen to his word with your ears, or do you listen to his word with your heart? Have you closed your eyes and ears to his teachings because of disillusionment, discouragement, and lack of results in your life?

God is looking for people who understand with their hearts, not their tickling ears, and who returned to him, back to his church, back to his teachings, back to the basics of his simple scriptures so that we may be healed by him.

We must analyze our hearts, we must analyze our intentions, we must analyze our priorities, we must analyze our value system, and we must analyze and evaluate our fellowship with God, our common union with the Holy Spirit, and our daily walk. I see so many Christians whose minds are clouded, whose bodies are sick, with no direction, no results, living in total hopelessness and not knowing why.

We must take our God and his holy word seriously. God did not pay the ultimate price through the ultimate sacrifice, through innocent, holy blood, for a nobody. We are God's ultimate gift, we are God's precious created beings, and we are the best thing that God has ever made. But because of sin, human beings have been alienated and separated from God, and even though human beings chose to be away and separated from God, our heavenly Father so loved us that he gave his only begotten son that whosoever would believe in him would not perish but have everlasting life (John 3:16).

The next answer is found in James 5:13–16:

> **Is anyone among you suffering? Let him pray. Is anyone cheerful? Let them sing praises. Is anyone among you sick? Let them call the elders of the church, and let them pray over him, anointing him with oil in the name of the Lord; and the prayer offered in faith will restore the one who is sick, and the Lord will raise him up, and if he has committed sins, they will be forgiven him. Therefore, confess your sins one to another, and pray one for another, so that you may be healed. The effectual prayer of a righteous man can accomplish much.**

One, we have to call the elders of the church. Two, the elders of the church have to know how to pray in faith. Three, he has to be anointed with oil. Four, he must humble himself. Five, he needs to analyze how many areas of his personal life he is grieving the Holy Spirit. Six, he must be humble enough to admit it. Seven, he must be humble enough to turn his back on whatever is grieving the Holy Spirit. Eight, he must not be judgmental of a brother or a minister that is trying to help him. Nine, he must be willing to turn around from what he is doing wrong and be willing to make changes.

In Psalm 107:17, it states that some were fools because of their rebellious way, and because of their iniquities, they were afflicted.

In John 8:31–32, it states that Jesus was saying to those Jews who had believed in him, "If you abide in my word, then you are truly disciples of mine; and you shall know the truth, and the truth shall make you free."

I have found that there is no humility among Christians and even in some pastors. I have tried praying for people, and they said to me, "I have already prayed, thank you very much," and their attitude has been high-minded.

These are people that don't even know what is happening in their lives, people that have a dreaded disease, people that are about to die, people that are waiting on transplants, and they say, "I have already prayed." So much arrogance, so much self-centeredness, I have even heard them say to me from the mouth of an actual pastor, "Oh, I go against all established order." Even while being in the hospital under a strict diet, they have asked me, "Go over to a fast-food restaurant and bring me a hamburger." Now, of course, they've been really cool about this. I have been there between thirty minutes to an hour and a half, and sisters from the church show up and say to the patient, "How are you? How are you doing?" And before the patient even says anything, they say, "You are in victory, right!"

Self-centeredness, arrogance, religiosity, stubbornness, and unteachable spirit—these are the greatest problem as to why a lot of people don't get healed. Every nonbeliever that people have asked me to go and pray for has gotten healed, while sixty percent of all the believers that I have prayed for, God has had a problem healing or delivering them because of their unteachable spirit. They know it all, and the best of all is this: they say to me, "I don't receive it." They are in denial. They don't admit that they have a problem, and they think that if they would admit it, they would be giving in to the devil.

There is no shame in being sick or needing someone to pray for you. Jesus said that any sick among you, let them call the elders of the church, anointing them with oil, and the prayer of faith shall save the sick, and if they have committed any sin, it will be forgiven (James 5:14).

If Jesus himself is telling us through the epistle of James to call the elders of the church to be prayed for, what is wrong with it?

Let's look at some obstacles. Why haven't I received healing?

Number 1, not understanding the "substitution," death, burial, and resurrection of our Lord Jesus Christ on our behalf.

Everything Jesus Christ came to do was to purchase us from the grip of the enemy, remove us from the slavery of that kingdom, and translate us into the kingdom of his dear Son.

In Colossians 2:12–15, it states,

> **And it says having been buried with him in baptism, in which you were also raised up with him through faith in the working of God, Who raised him from the dead. And when you were dead in your transgressions and the un-circumcision of your flesh, He made you alive together with him, having forgiven us all our transgressions, having canceled out the certificate of debt consisting of decrees against us and which was hostile to us; and he has taken it out of the way, having nailed it to the cross. When he had disarmed the rulers and authorities, he made a public display of them, having triumphed over them through him.**

Even in our transgressions, he had already made us alive together with him, so when we received Jesus Christ, that being made alive was manifested in our hearts and lives. Can you see it?

Our being made alive was purchased for us on the cross 2,013 years ago, and the moment we accept the free gift of eternal life, we have passed from death unto life so that we may live a resurrected life according to the scriptures in Colossians 3:1.

Every Christian purchased by the blood of Jesus Christ has been buried with him in baptism, and we were also raised up with him through faith by the work of God, who raised Jesus from the dead and has completely delivered us from the grip of sin, the curse of the law, and the bondage that the enemy put upon us. We are free, we are free, we are free! Say that out loud. Say it again.

Say it again, pass the information from your lips down to your heart and believe it with your heart. When you start saying things like this, you start with your intellect, and the words come out of your mouth. And the more you say them, the more you repeat them, the more your lips will connect to your heart, and you start believing it in your heart.

Right now, raise both of your arms to the sky and say, "Heavenly Father, I thank you that through the blood of the Lord Jesus Christ, you paid for my sin and you delivered me from sickness, disease, and infirmity, which is the slavery of the devil and his demons, and right now I apply that precious blood from the crown of my head to the soles of my feet, and I call upon your resurrection power to well up within me as a river of living water and invade this entire atmosphere. Right now, Holy Spirit, I invite you to saturate the atmosphere in this room, to saturate my mind, to saturate my body. Oh, heavenly Father, I want to enter into the Holy of Holies and have communion with you in Jesus's name, amen."

I don't know if you sense that, but I did; the precious Holy Spirit is in this room. Notice in verse 13 that while we were yet sinners in the uncircumcision of our flesh, we were already made alive together with him. Remember, this happened 2,013 years ago, having forgiven us all our transgressions. Imagine not having even been born again, and yet we were already made alive, and our transgressions had already been forgiven. How much more now that we have passed from death unto life and we are born-again Christians? Can you see it?

The curse pronounced in Adam and Eve was called the certificate of debt, consisting of decrees found in verse 14 that was hostile against us. He has taken it out of the way and nailed it to the cross, then he defeated principalities and powers and rules of this dark age, found in verse 15, making a public display, triumphing over them through him. So, my brother and my sister, isn't this self-explanatory? Aren't you already jumping on your own two feet? Right now, get up on your feet, say with your lips out loud, "Devil, get out of my life, get out of my mind, get out of my body, get out of my blood." Lay your hands on the part of your body that you need divine healing or deliverance and say, "Devil, I bind you, I rebuke you, and I command you to get out right now, in Jesus's name. Get out of my house, out of my relationships, get out of my family, get out of my finances, in Jesus's name, amen."

More on going into the Holy of Holies in the name of Jesus Christ and accessing God's supernatural power, which is the manifestation of his precious Holy Spirit further on.

Now if you are not born again, but have had only a religious experience, you need to get born again, and this is how it is done.

Right now, say out loud, "God Almighty, I know that I am a sinner and I cannot save myself. My religion won't save me, my sacrificial dos and don'ts won't save me, my tradition won't save me. I repent of my sin. I turn my back on sin. Lord Jesus, right now come into my life, save me, and fill me with the Holy Spirit, amen." My friend, my brother, if you have prayed that prayer, I believe you've become born again. You are a new creation (1 Corinthians 5:17). This is where you can find exactly what happened in your life just now.

Now I know that from now on, everything you keep on reading in this book you will understand it with new insight and divine revelation.

Number 2, not understanding the "mediation" and "propitiation" between God and man.

When Jesus Christ died on the cross, was buried, and on the third day rose again, he went up into heaven, took his precious blood, sprinkled it on the mercy seat, and said, "Father, this is my blood, which has been shed for the remission of sin and paying for eternal redemption once and for all that your righteous judgment demanded from human beings." Then he sat at the right hand of the Father to become the mediator until this day since he always lives to make intercessions for us (Hebrews 10:12–14).

In 1 John 2:1–2, it reads,

> **My little children, I am writing these things do you that you may not sin. And if anyone sins, we have an advocate with the father, Jesus Christ the righteous; and he himself is the propitiation for our sins; and not for ours only, but also for those of the whole world.**

In Hebrews 7:25, it states,

> **Hence, also, He is able to save forever those who draw near to God through him, since he always lives to make intercession for them.**

He not only died on the cross for us to take upon himself the sins of the world, and that's you and me, but he also took his precious blood to the altar of the mercy seat in heaven and obtained eternal redemption, eternal forgiveness, eternal acceptance, and eternal reconciliation. He mediated as a lawyer would for us. He was the propitiation in our behalf. He did it because he loves us. He did it because this is what he came to do. He did not come to teach us religious dos and don'ts; he came to mediate and to take upon himself what we deserve, the judgment and curse for our disobedience and rebellion. He died in our place to take upon himself the righteous judgment of a holy God. That is why he said, "My father, my father, why hast thou forsaken me?" He said that while on the cross; the judgment of God for all human beings was upon his shoulders at that time.

What we all deserved was put upon him at that time so all of us could be free, so all of us could be delivered and set free, so all of us could be released for the judgment of God and the condemnation of the enemy.

He did not only mediate for us. He was the propitiation for us (but he is now our heavenly lawyer seated at the right hand of the Father, daily interceding for us). Please think about this—we are always striving to look for money so that a lawyer could represent us in a court of law, yet we have a heavenly lawyer who intercedes for us day and night to assure us that the covenant right he purchased for us on the cross would be fulfilled. Just on this promise alone, I am shouting happily, jumping up and down, and appropriating his precious blood daily upon my mind, my body, my relationships, my whole family, and everything I touch.

So you see, my brother. Can you see this, my sister? We are not to be bound; we are not in slavery. We have been set free by the precious blood of Jesus Christ shed on the cross.

In 1 Peter 3:22, it states,

> **Who is at the right hand of God, having gone into heaven, after angels and authorities and powers had been subjected to him.**

Number 3, not knowing "justification."

In Galatians 2:16–18, it reads,

> **Nevertheless knowing that a man is not justified by the works of the law but through faith in Christ Jesus, even we have believed in Christ Jesus, that we may be justified by faith in Christ, and not by the works of all law; since by the works of the law shall no flesh be justified.**

We bow our heads and receive Jesus Christ as our Lord and Savior; we are accepting what he did on our behalf so that his precious blood makes us right and just in the sight of Almighty God.

Not by works so that no man would boost, there is a positional justification attributed to every believer, not by works, but as a gift, and then there is living a just life, which we'll talk about on. We must understand the gift first and what we are in Christ. Then we will work on what we have to do in Christ.

In Galatians 3:7–16, this is what it says:

> **Therefore, be sure that it is those who are of faith who are sons of Abraham. And the Scripture, foreseeing that God would justify the Gentiles by faith, preached the gospel beforehand to Abraham, saying, "All the nations shall be blessed in you."**

Notice here that God preached the gospel to Abraham for the justification of the Gentiles, that's you and me, through faith in Jesus, who was not a physical descendant of the bloodline of the Israeli people. God said that every Gentile that would accept the Lordship of Jesus Christ shall be blessed with Abraham in Abraham's seed, which is Jesus, shall all the nations of the world be blessed, and this is a promise that should get us all happy and jumping up and down.

We have covered in this book how blessed Abraham was, which is our inheritance.

So then those who are of faith are blessed with Abraham, the believer. For us, many as are of the works of the law are under a curse; for it is written, "Cursed is everyone who does not abide by all the things written in the book of the law, to perform them." Now that no one is justified by the law before God is evident; for, "A righteous man shall live by faith."

Now understand that only those who walk in faith, with a justified life through the shed blood of Jesus, are the only ones being blessed. Every other individual, whether it be a Gentile, a Jew, an Arab, an Oriental, or any other culture, or any other religion, according to verse 10, is under a curse, for it is written, "Cursed is everyone who does not abide by all the things written in the book off the law, to perform them." Now remember, I didn't write this; God did.

In order to receive our supernatural deliverance from evil spirits or live in divine health, we must understand what somebody else died in our place and has freely given to us by faith. When we received him as our Lord and Savior, all these benefits came with him and were attributed to us. Every blessing Abraham received is ours. Abraham lived a long and healthy life; therefore, we should live a long and healthy life. It is our inheritance paid for by the blood of Jesus Christ.

Justification is the gift of God, not of works; there are no religious dos or don'ts that we can do to be righteous. Verse 11 says, "A Righteous man shall live by faith."

Say with me out loud, "Heavenly Father, we come to you in Jesus Christ, asking you to forgive us for trying to justify our lives based on works, based on religious dos and don'ts, and not through faith in the total work of Calvary through the shed blood of the Lord Jesus Christ in our behalf." Raise both of your arms to the sky, and say out loud, "We have been substituted, mediated for, made propitiation for, and justified by the precious blood of Jesus. He took away our sins on the cross. He took away sicknesses and diseases on the cross. Therefore, we call upon his precious Holy Spirit to deliver us right now, from the crown of our head to the soles of our feet, from every illegal trespasser that has trespassed on to God's property, for we have been redeemed from the curse of the law and made righteous, which is right standing before God Almighty through our mediator Jesus Christ, amen."

We no longer belong to us. We have been bought and paid for; therefore, we belong to God, and we have been made God's holy temple. No unholy thing should trespass, jump on, or enslave the property and temple of Almighty God.

We must take what we are reading, sit back, and meditate on it until it materializes in our lives. Our spirit, our mind, and our body should be completely made whole and healthy.

However, the law is not of faith; on the contrary, "He who practices them shall live by them." Christ redeemed us from the curse of the law, having become a curse for us-for it is written, "Cursed is everyone who hangs on a tree." In order that in Christ Jesus the blessings of Abraham might come to the Gentiles so that we might receive the promise of the spirit through faith. Brethren, I speak in terms of human relations: even through it is only man's covenant, yet when it has been ratified, no one set-aside or ads conditions to it. Now the promises were spoken to Abraham and to his seed. He does not say, "And to seeds," as referring to many, but rather to one, "And to your seed," that is, Christ.

The seed of Abraham was Isaac, the seed of Isaac was Jacob, and so on, all the way to Jesus Christ. That is why it says in verse 16, "And to your seed, that is, Christ." When you and I accept Jesus Christ of Nazareth's death, burial, and resurrection on our behalf as a substitution Lamb that takes away the sins of all the world, you and I are part of the world. We are inserted into the family of Abraham, becoming an heir with Christ. Delivering us from the curse of the law upon both the Jews and Gentiles, which we have tried to be just in the eyes of God through religious dos and don'ts, and also some rituals from the law of Moses. If we believe only in order to receive, the blessings of Abraham will come upon Jews as well as Gentiles.

Number 4, not knowing there is a new law called "the law of faith."

In Romans 3:20, it says,

> **Because by the works of the law no flesh will be justified in his sight; for through the law comes the knowledge of sin. But now apart from the law the righteousness of God has been manifested, being witnessed by the law and the prophets, even the righteousness of God through faith in Jesus Christ for all those who believe; for there is no distinction.**

I have to say something here that is very important. Even the righteousness of God through faith in Jesus Christ for those who believe, the righteousness of God imputed, the righteousness of God attributed, the righteousness of God as a free gift, not through works, not through good deeds when Jesus enters your body, you are made righteous in the sight of God. In order to understand being set free and divine health, we must understand who we are in Christ.

In 2 Corinthians 5:21, the Bible says,

> **He made him who knew no sin, to be sin in our behalf, that we might become the righteousness of God in him.**

In Christ, we have been made as righteous as God. That is really hard to believe because we are constantly justifying ourselves before God through what we do. In Christ, we have been made the righteousness of God. Without works, if not, it is not of faith.

I needed to inject this before we went to verse 23 because our greatest job in life is passing all this information from our head and bringing it down sixteen inches into our hearts, for this will be the only way we will receive our inheritance. Notice this in verse 24.

For all have sinned and fallen short of the glory of God, being justified as a gift by his grace through the redemption which is in Christ Jesus, whom God displayed publicly as a propitiation in his blood through faith. This was to demonstrate his righteousness because, in the forbearance of God, he passed over the sins previously committed; for the demonstration, I say, of his righteousness at the present time, that he might be just and the justifier of the one who has faith in Jesus.

Aren't you jumping up and down yet? Being justified as a gift by grace, through redemption, which means being bought and paid for by the blood of Jesus Christ through faith. Can't you see that you will never be just based on what you do? Can't you see the words "free gift through faith"? Can't you see the words "through redemption"? It is all done through faith.

God had to demonstrate his righteousness imputed upon us through our faith in the Lordship of Jesus Christ. Every sin in the past, every sin in the present, and every sin we will ever commit in the future has been taken care of by Christ on the cross.

In verse 27, where then is boasting? It is excluded. By what kind of law? Of works? No, but by a law of faith. Can you see the new law of faith working here?

For we maintain that a man is justified by faith apart from works of the law. Or is God the God of the Jews only? Is he not the God of the Gentiles also? Yes, of Gentiles also.

I'm so glad that he is not only the God of the Jews but also the God of the Gentiles.

Jesus Christ the just, justifying the sinner. Now let's look at what the apostle Paul has to say.

In Philippians 3:9, the apostle Paul says,

And may be found in him, not having a righteousness of my own derived from the law, but that which is through faith in Christ, the righteousness which comes from God on the basis of faith. That I may know him, and the power of his resurrection and the fellowship of his suffering, being conformed to his death; in order that I may obtain to the resurrection from the dead.

The apostle Paul was a converted Jew from the works of the law to the saving grace of Jesus Christ, and then he himself said in verse 9, "Not having a righteousness of my own derived from the law." Notice he's not talking about righteousness based on works, sacrificial lambs, or any other ritual of the law, but the righteousness that is through faith in Jesus Christ. Now if an Israeli needed to be justified through faith in Jesus Christ, what about us Gentiles, who have over ten thousand gods?

Under the dispensation of grace, which God himself made through Jesus Christ up until now, there is no escape. We all have to come to God through Christ by faith, faith in the total work of Christ on Calvary.

Christians around the world are privileged people because Jesus Christ himself did all the work on the cross for us so that we would be free and enjoy our fellowship with God through him and live in the victory that Jesus himself paid for.

Not understanding who has already come inside us and what he has brought with himself in order for us to be whole in spirit, soul, and body causes a lot of us to be discouraged, disillusioned, and powerless to believe what is right. Despite the fact that we have a covenant right to be healthy, the enemy still trespasses against God's property, which is us, and tries to influence, tries to torment, tries to put sickness and disease upon us. There is a big difference between your covenant right, your daily fellowship with God through prayer and the reading of the Word, and your daily relationship with human beings on this earth.

No born-again Spirit-filled Christian can be demon possessed or generationally cursed. It is impossible. The Holy Spirit and demon spirits cannot invade the same house. We have received Jesus Christ of Nazareth by faith. We have received his rights and privileges by faith. He lives inside our body in the person of the Holy Spirit, taking up residence for himself, thereby causing us to be his holy temple.

Now I have seen a lot of Christians who are not committed to Christ, who are not his daily disciples, whose minds are clouded, whose bodies are sick, and without direction in their lives, and the question is, "Why am I in this hopeless situation?" I hear a lot of Christians saying, "I wonder what the will of God is for my life." And these questions are sad.

And you look at a Bible. It is God's holy Word. It is God's holy covenant for us. It is God's testament. The word "testament" means "will." How can we say, "I wonder what the will of God is for my life"?

We have the will of God. We have his commitment, which is his covenant to bless us, and the only prerequisite is faith, faith in the written Word of God, faith in the promises of God, and faith in his commitment to abide by his word because our God never changes. He is not a liar. He is not a man that he should repent. He covenanted with us and left us sixty-six books. Which of them do we not believe?

In Matthew 7:7, it states,

> **Ask, and it shall be given to you; seek, and you shall find; knock, and it shall be opened unto you.**

These are powerful words spoken by the God man.

In John 1:14, it states,

> **And the word became flesh and we beheld his glory, glory as the only begotten of the father full of grace and truth.**

When we hold the Bible, we hear Jesus Christ himself say, "Ask, and it shall be given you; seek, and you shall find; knock, and it shall be opened unto you." These are very powerful words that should not be taken lightly.

First, understand what these powerful words mean. Ask, he wants us to ask, and the answer to your asking is found in the written Word of God. The New Testament is the new covenant established by better promises through the shed blood of Jesus Christ, once and for all. We can ask God through prayer in Jesus's name for whatever it is we want.

Second, he said for us to seek. Seek what? Exactly what it is we need. Now where do we seek? In his covenant, of course, his Word, his written word, not elsewhere, but his Word, not the advice of a preacher, not the advice of a friend, not the advice of a wife. I am not against any one of these, but he said to seek your answer in his written Word. The Word of God has an answer to every human problem, every human need, every human shortcoming.

Third, knock, and it shall be opened unto you. Here we don't see him saying, "Maybe." We see words like, "and it shall be done," "it shall," and "you shall receive." We have to learn to receive the covenanted blessings of God through faith in the Lord Jesus Christ. It is what he came to do, to open the way for us to enter into God's holy throne in heaven. We can all come to God through Jesus and receive from God everything we need.

Being set free from influence, from oppression, from tormenting demonic power is our God-given right.

We have the Constitution of the United States of America, full of constitutional rights and privileges, but once in a while, we are influenced, tormented, or bound by some deceiving, lying thief who wants to take our legal rights, our identity, and what is legally ours, our possessions. Aren't we truly blessed to live in such a country as the United States of America? God bless America.

We have the constitution of the kingdom of heaven, established in our hearts, full of constitutional rights and privileges, but the enemy is constantly throwing fiery darts at us, wanting to influence us, wanting to torment us, and in some cases, binding some of us. He wants to take away our legal rights, our identity, and what is legally ours, including our possessions. Aren't we truly blessed that we are citizens of a greater kingdom? Our citizenship is in heaven, and we have a new flag to pledge allegiance to, and that is the Christian flag.

When we read God's holy constitution and receive our heavenly lawyer as our only Lord and Savior, we are born into the greatest living organism on the face of this planet, and all his rights and privileges that are there written belong to us. It's like being a United States citizen and not claiming your rights and privileges given to us by the Constitution, so why be a citizen?

Why be a Christian? Why be born again? Why enter into this holy organism called the government of the Lord Jesus Christ? Why become a member of his body? Why be baptized in the Holy Spirit to receive power over the enemy? Why have heavenly citizenship? Why not believe God's holy constitution, his holy covenant, his holy testament, and his holy Word through the new law of faith?

Faith—not emotionalism, not body ruled, not the lust of the eye, not the lust of the flesh, not the pride of life—should govern our lives (1 John 2:15–16).

> **Do not love the world, nor the things in the world. If anyone loves the world, the love of the father is not in him. For all that is in the world, the lust of the flesh of the lust of the eyes and the pride of life, is not from the father, but is from the world.**

In these verses, we are told not to love the world or the things that are in the world. Our eyes are very lustful; they lust for a lot of things—relationships, material things, careers, and ministry.

Our bodies are very lustful. In Galatians 5:19–21, there is a list of the things that our body lusts for. Apart from that list, I'm going to say three others: Number 1, our body lusts after sex. Number 2, our body lusts the bed; it doesn't want to get up. Number 3, our body lusts after food. If we are governed by our flesh, we are doomed to fail; our body is one of our worst enemies.

And the boastful pride of life, Hollywood, glory, glamour, the possession of things, eloquence, status, position, and many other things that are very boastful and prideful.

These are our greatest enemies of faith. Faith in Jesus Christ and total health for our bodies.

In Luke 4:18–19, it states,

> **The spirit of the Lord is upon me because he has anointed me to preach the gospel to the poor. He has sent me to proclaim release to the captives, and recovery of sight to the blind, to set free those who are downtrodden, to proclaim the favorable year of the Lord.**

Notice here the original intent as to why Jesus Christ of Nazareth came into the world. He was anointed, which means full of the Holy Spirit, to preach the gospel to the poor, which is any human being that has not been born again or has not been full of the Holy Spirit in this world.

Deliverance to the captives. Are we captive? Are we bound? Are we enslaved by the enemy? Jesus Christ came to give us good news, to destroy the works of the enemy in our lives. Sickness, disease, and infirmity are the works of the enemy upon us. Jesus came to take it away and destroy the works of the enemy in our lives. To give us spiritual insight, to heal our blindness, to give us divine revelation of God's holy word.

To set free those that are downtrodden. Are we downtrodden? Are we bound by any disease or infirmity? Do we feel out and out? Are we hanging on to a promise? Let's believe his word right now. Let's make today the favorable year of the Lord in our lives. Let's stop hoping and trusting in the future, and let us start believing it already happened on the cross on our behalf. And then demand the enemy to leave our bodies, in Jesus's name.

Under this new dispensation of grace, which is unmerited favor from God, every Christian walks by faith, not by sight (Hebrews 10:38).

Number 5, not honoring God's anointed

In Matthew 10:1, it states,

> **And having summoned his 12 disciples, He gave them authority over unclean spirits, to cast them out, and to heal every kind of disease and every kind of sicknesses. "And as you go, preach, saying, the kingdom of heaven is at hand. Heal the sick, raise the dead, cleanse the lepers, cast out demons; freely you received, freely give. Do not acquire gold, or silver, or copper for your money belts, or a bag for your journey, or even two tunics, or sandals, or a staff; for the worker is worthy of his support. And whoever does not receive you, nor heed your words, as you call out of that house or that city, shake off the dust of your feet. Truly I say to you, it will be more tolerable for the land of Sodom and Gomorrah in the Day of Judgment, than for that city."**

Dishonoring the man of God, dishonoring a brother who is appointed and anointed, dishonoring a preacher, not accepting their calling or the fact that they were chosen for a particular cause in the body of Christ, we see in these passages that Jesus commissioned his twelve, and he gave them strict orders to preach that the kingdom of heaven is at hand and to heal the sick, to raise the dead, to cleanse the lepers, and to cast out demons. And in verse 14, he said, "Whoever does not receive you, nor heed your words, shake off the dust of your feet because for that person or that city it will be worse than Sodom and Gomorrah in the day of judgment."

There have been many people who came to me for prayer, especially the Christians, but because I'm not a well-known evangelist around the world, they don't honor me as they should, but if they hear that a well-known evangelist is going to be in town, they run to that crusade, get prayed on, and come back the same way they went in, not healed, and they spent between $25 and $300 that night.

We should never disregard the prayer of the simple. We should always honor every single prayer that a willing heart is willing to do on our behalf. You never know what miracle God could do through that simple person, and we must always honor every single person that is anointed of God.

Number 6, disregarding grace and going back to tradition.

In Galatians 4:8–11, it says,

> **However, at that time, when you did not know God, you were slaves to those which by nature are not gods. But now that you have come to know God, or rather to be known by God, how is it that you turn back again to the weak and worthless elemental things, to which you desire to be enslaved all over again? You observed days and months and seasons and years. I fear for you, that perhaps I have labored over you in vain.**

When a Christian who has tasted being born again, being filled with the Holy Spirit, and even has experienced divine healing and backslides to the weak and feeble things of this world, it is often very hard for them to be prayed for in order to get healed.

I know a lot of Christians that are looking at magazines and following the horoscopes. Some of them are going to different salons and practicing yoga. Others are practicing karate. Others are practicing the religion of their fathers or the religion of their wives. I see them picking up eggs on Easter Sunday with their kids. Others are observing Halloween. Others are not even going to church, and others are mixing the godly teachings written in the Word of God with oriental philosophies taught by Buddha.

In verse 8, it says, "Slaves to those who by nature are not gods." These brothers and sisters have been known by God, but they have turned back to weak and worthless elements, things to which they desire to be enslaved all over again.

In verse 10, they observed days and months and seasons and years instead of reading the book of Proverbs to get the supernatural wisdom from heaven or reading the book of Ecclesiastes so they may know what are the things of eternal value to live by, or even the Psalms to learn how to pray and to learn how to humble themselves before God Almighty and in Jesus Christ get the answer to their prayers and the results for their lives that they so desperately need. Some are smoking, drinking, dancing, and in disobedience to God's word.

Even the apostle Paul here is concerned that his teaching and sharing of the holy word of God with these Galatians would have been in vain, dishonoring the grace of God. It's a very dangerous thing to do, for the Bible says there is no more sacrifice for sin.

In Galatians 5:1–4, it states,

> **It was for freedom that Christ set us free; therefore keep standing firm and do not be subject again to a yoke of slavery. Behold I, Paul, say to you that if you receive circumcision, Christ will be of no benefit to you. And I testify again to every man who receives circumcision, that he is under obligation to keep the whole law. You have been severed from Christ, you who are seeking to be justified by law; you have fallen from grace.**

This is very dangerous backsliding to the weak and feeble things of this world and consciously rejecting the precious holy blood of Jesus shed on Calvary for our justification, our redemption, and our wholeness in spirit, soul, and body. Notice what it says here that if we practice any one of these rituals (in this particular passage in verse 2, it talked about circumcision), Christ will be of no benefit to us. If you are Jewish and you are reading this book, and you try to practice anything of the law, Christ will be of no benefit to you, or if you are a Gentile and you are practicing any one of these horoscopes or oriental religions, Christ will be of no benefit to you.

In verse 4, it says that we have been severed from Christ. Those of us who will try to be justified by the works of the law or by practicing any other philosophies, we can fall from grace.

Contrary to a lot of Calvinists, some messianic Jews, Seventh-day Adventists, or any other religious practices that are mixing justification by works and justification by grace, according to what we just read, we can fall from grace. And in the following verses, I will show you that the wrath of God will come upon those who continually mix grace and law, grace and works, and grace and other philosophies and are not totally committed to following in the footsteps of Jesus as his disciple. We must look very carefully at what the following teaching Will illuminate as with and the danger, of backsliding, to other philosophies. In this particular passage, the letter is being written to the Jewish people who wanted to go back to the law and to practice traditional rituals of the law and backslide from the knowledge of grace.

Now in, Hebrews 10:15–19, it states,

> **And the Holy Spirit also bears witness to us; for after saying, "This is the covenant that I will make with them after those days says the Lord: I will put my laws upon their heart, And upon their mind I will write them," He then says, "And their sins and their lawless deeds I will remember no more." Now where there is forgiveness of these things, there is no longer any offering for sin. Since therefore,**

> **brethren, we have confidence to enter into the holy place by the blood of Jesus, by a new and living way which he inaugurated for us through the veil, that is, his flesh, and since we have a great priest over the house of God, let us draw near with a sincere heart in full assurance of faith, having our hearts sprinkled clean from all evil conscience and our bodies washed with pure water. Let us hold fast the confession of our hope without wavering, for he who promised is faithful: and let us consider how to stimulate one another to love and good deeds, not forsaking our own assembling together, as it is the habit of some, but encouraging one another, and all the more, as you see the day drawing near. For if we go on sinning willfully after receiving the knowledge of the truth, there no longer remains a sacrifice for sins, but a certain terrifying expectation of judgment, and the fury of a fire which will consume the adversaries.**

I am not going to read the entire book of Hebrews to explain to the readers that these misunderstood verses have been taken out of context by a lot of people around the world.

It is not talking about the born-again believer who is filled with the Holy Spirit who has fallen and who, not knowing by ignorance, has said something, has done something, or has not done something and that there is no more forgiveness for their sin. Every new bornagain babe in Christ is learning to walk with our heavenly Father as a child, is learning to renew his mind, is learning how to read the Word, and is learning how to walk in the Spirit so that he will not fulfill the lust of the flesh and many other things that we do out of ignorance or by immaturity. These verses only apply—and please listen to this very carefully—to those people who tasted a born-again experience, who tasted having a Spirit-filled life and then turned their backs by backsliding to the weak and feeble things of this world and the religious dos and don'ts of the past.

We must understand that we are under a new dispensation of grace, with unmerited favor, thanks to the death, burial, and resurrection of our Lord and Savior Jesus Christ, that while in our development of spiritual growth and fellowship with the Father, we're going to make a lot of mistakes that are under the blood already, because when God elected us and called us, he knew beforehand about our imperfect nature, and that is why he instituted a new covenant of grace.

Now for those people who were truly born again and filled with the Holy Spirit but disgracefully rejected the blood of Jesus Christ and went back to their old religion to practice dos and don'ts in their religion, that person has trodden down on the blood of the Lord Jesus Christ, and verse 27 calls them the adversary. Now for those people, a terrifying expectation of judgment and a fiery fury from God will come upon them. Those people under this judgment are seeking to be healed in their bodies. Their minds are confused. They have no direction for their lives, and when we Christians try to pray for them, a lot of times, they do not get healed because God is trying to get their attention through this particular challenge and they are not listening.

His precious covenant has been shed in our hearts, and as we read his holy Word, he will write his word in our mind, and our sins he will remember no more. Where there is forgiveness of these things, there is no longer any offering for sin.

You can imagine the confidence that we can have in entering the holy place of Almighty God through the blood of the Lord Jesus Christ by the new and living way, which he opened up for us through his flesh. Have you any idea what we are talking about? That through the shed blood of our Lord and Savior Jesus Christ, every born-again believer has his covenant in our hearts, and his word is written in our mind, and we have access to the throne room of Almighty God, hallelujah.

Every born-again believer has a high priest seated at the right hand of the Father. Why would we want to go back to those dead and feeble ways and backslide to dead gods when we have access to the Creator of the sun the moon and the sky? And he loves us. Why are we going to talk to those idols that have eyes but cannot see, that have ears but cannot hear, that have a nose but cannot breathe, that have arms but cannot feel, that have legs but cannot run? Why are we going to disgracefully reject the grace of Almighty God through the shed blood of the Lord Jesus Christ?

If you have wandered off from faith in the Lordship of Jesus Christ, you have been lied to and deceived by the enemy. Right now say, "Heavenly Father, I repent of my sin, and I turn my back on these idols and these oriental philosophies. I turn my back on these horoscopes. I turn my back on every occult activity that I have been practicing, and I ask you right now to cleanse me with the precious blood of Jesus. From the crown of my head to the soles of my feet, destroy every work of the enemy on my mind. Lord Jesus, come into my heart, fill me with your precious Holy Spirit, be real to me today, have mercy upon my ignorance, and set me free in Jesus's name, amen."

If you said that prayer and you meant that from the bottom of your heart, God is there meeting you right at the point of your need. Now you can lay hands on yourself, and in the name of Jesus Christ of Nazareth, you can pray for yourself and ask God anything and he will do it for you. The sin of disgracefulness is the worst of all sins you can commit, ignorantly rejecting the blood of Jesus.

I can assure you that we will get to the bottom as to why a lot of people haven't received their healing. We will analyze as many doctrinal errors as possible and also human mistakes that we make, which are some of the reasons why some people haven't received their healing.

Number 7, not walking in love, two new commandments

In Matthew 22:34–40, it states,

> **But when the Pharisees heard that he had put the Sadducees to silence, they gathered themselves together. And one of them, a lawyer, asked him a question, testing him, "Teacher, which is the great commandment in the law?" And he said to him, "You shall love the Lord your God with all of your heart, with all of your soul, and with all of your**

mind. This is the great and foremost commandment. The second is like it, 'you shall love your neighbor as yourself.' On these two commandments depend the whole law and the prophets."

The Pharisees and the Sadducees were silenced by Jesus Christ because of their religiosity and their lack of love for human beings. Oh, yes, they were very religious people, but without love toward God and without love toward human beings, we can do absolutely nothing. Everybody at that time was testing Jesus, and all of us Christians will be tested to see how much we love God and how much we love people.

If we're going to receive the best from God, we must learn to walk in obedience to these two commandments. The first question would be, "How much do I love the Lord?" In these passages, it is very clear that Jesus is not asking us, but he is telling us that we should love God with three things—with all our heart, with all our soul, and with our entire mind.

I have always wondered why the Lord Jesus Christ used the word "all"—with all our heart. It is definitely implying that our hearts can be loving God and also loving something else. Our priorities could be completely out of order and, therefore, be divided. We must evaluate our hearts and ask ourselves, do we truly love God? Are we truly grateful for Jesus Christ on the cross? Are we truly thankful that he shed his precious blood on the cross to pay for our sin and guilt?

God, through Jesus, is ordering us to love him with all our hearts and not be divided between God and career, between God and the sports, between God and family, or between God and anything else.

Our soul is emotions, knowledge, and free will; we need to love our heavenly Father with our emotions. There is nothing wrong with being emotionally excited about our heavenly Father. Some people criticize African Americans because they are too emotionally excited about their God. What is wrong with it?

We must store as much knowledge of him as possible, read his Word daily, go to Bible studies, and obtain as much knowledge of him so that we may be transformed by the renewing of our minds (Romans 12:2).

We should all make the right choices for him. A lot of us make choices and put God second, third, or fourth in our list of things to do. Sometimes our priorities are television and becoming a couch potato, and then only we would come to God through prayer if we have a problem, a need, or we need something for our families, or sometimes only when we say grace. We need to make our heavenly Father a priority in the morning and late in the evening.

And then we need to love him with our entire mind. What is our thought life like? Do we think about our God daily in what we say, in what we do, in our thought life? Do we even remember God between Monday and Saturday, or do we only remember him on Sunday?

He said this is the great and foremost commandment.

He said the second is like it: "You shall love your neighbor as yourself."

Which brings me to the question, how much do we truly love ourselves?

Do we respect our heavenly Father? Do we respect his holy Word? Do we respect his preachers? Do we respect our soul? Do we respect our mind? Do we respect our bodies? Do we respect America? Do we respect everything that is of eternal value?

How is our self-worth? How is our self-value? What is it that we think about ourselves? How do we love ourselves? Once we get the answer to those questions, then we will be able to love our neighbor as we love ourselves.

It is very important to take seriously everything we have written in this book because they are our God-given rights and privileges, and we should not take them for granted.

Not walking in love toward our heavenly Father and not walking in love toward our fellow man, it's one of the greatest reasons why we are not physically healed in our bodies. The Bible says if you come to the altar and you remember that you have fought with your brother, leave your offering there, go back and reconcile with your brother, and then bring your offering (Matthew 5:23–24).

Our love for God, brothers and sisters, is a commandment and is not open for debate.

In 1 Thessalonians 4:6, it states,

> **And that no man transgress and defraud his brother in the matter because the Lord is the avenger in all these things, just as we also told you before and solemnly warned you.**

If we read from verse 1 to verse 12, we will see that this is the perfect will of God for our lives.

> **For God has not called us for the purpose of impurity but in sanctification.**

We need to walk as saints of God and not transgressing and defrauding our brothers.

Our relationship with God depends on how much we love him and how much of him is within us through the baptism in the Holy Spirit so that the fruit of the Spirit, which is love, may be manifested vertically toward God and horizontally toward men. At the end of the day, we should look, act, and behave like Jesus Christ of Nazareth, our Lord and our Savior. He is our mirror to look to and evaluate our thought life, our conversations, and our conduct toward our brothers and the human beings in general.

When we read 1 Thessalonians 4:6, sometimes we take that word very lightly while we don't really even look into the meaning of that word. I looked up a *Webster* dictionary because I was really curious what it really meant, and it was amazing what I found under the word "avenger."

It says, number 1, "to take vengeance or exact exemplary punishment for, in behalf of a person or persons"; number 2, "to inflict revenge upon, as for an act of insult"; number 3, "to take vengeance, or punish, retaliate, revenge, vindicate, and visit." To "avenge" is to visit some offense with fitting punishment; to "revenge" is to inflict harm or suffering upon another through personal anger and resentment. Can you see how far the Lord will go to avenge us from the wrong our brothers and sisters will do to us daily? The apostle Paul is trying to warn us that God Almighty will take care of his children and fight in our behalf.

So we must be very careful to examine our hearts to see how we are treating our brothers and sisters in the Lord, because God will protect them from us also and chastise us.

Aren't you glad that we do not have to fight our battles with our brothers and sisters? All we have to do is bring them to God in prayer, and God himself will take care of them. That is a relief to me. I don't have to fight; just love everybody and God will take care of the rest.

Do you remember what God did to Cain and how the innocent blood of Abel cried out to the sky? God heard that innocent blood had been shed on the ground.

Do you remember what God did to Pharaoh when the innocent blood of the Jewish people was being shed on the ground and how God himself fought for the well-being of the children of Israel?

A lot of Christians are fighting the devil. A lot of Christians are saying, "Wow, look at what the devil is doing against me." They are running constantly from the enemy's attacks, and at the end of the day, it is God himself avenging the people they have transgressed or defrauded, holding back all his blessings and holding back his favor. And sometimes they even say, "My business is cursed. I see no results. Nothing goes well. Everything I touch falls apart. I wonder where is God and what is he doing. How come he doesn't love me? How come he doesn't answer my prayers?" Truly, the only thing we need to do is check and evaluate our hearts in regard to our relationship with our brothers, especially those that are younger in the Lord, for we might have become stumbling blocks.

Our goal in this book is not to find faults and failures in the lives of Christians, but that we may evaluate our lives and evaluate our walk and relationship with other people, which is really, at the end of the day, the things that are holding back the hand of God to bless our lives and heal our bodies.

Number 8, taking the Lord's supper in an unworthy manner.

In 1 Corinthians 11:23–32, it states,

> **For I received from the Lord that which I also delivered to you, but the Lord Jesus in the night in which he was betrayed took bread; and when he had given thanks, He broke it, and said, "This is my body, which is for you; do this in remembrance of me." In the same way He took the cup also, after supper, saying, "This cup is the new covenant in my blood; do this, as often as you drink it, in remembrance of me." For as often as you eat this bread and drink the cup, you proclaim the Lord's death until he comes. Therefore whoever eats the bread or drinks the cup of the Lord in an unworthy manner, shall be guilty of the body and the blood of the Lord. But let a man examine himself, and so let him eat of the bread and drink of the cup. For he who eats and drinks, eats and drinks judgment to himself, if he does not judge the body rightly. For this reason many among you are weak and sick, and a number sleep. But if we judge ourselves rightly, we should not be judged. But when we are judged, we are disciplined by the Lord in order that we may not be condemned along with the world.**

Here we see a perfect scenario of what is happening in a lot of churches and why they are not being healed: they are weak, they are sick, and they are dying.

When we go to church and they are preparing to take communion, even if the preacher does not teach on the Lord's body and on the Lord's blood from the Old Testament and from the New Testament, we need to ask ourselves, do we really know what we're doing? These verses are self-explanatory, and it doesn't require a lot of teaching or preaching on the topic, just a careful examination of our relationship with God through Jesus Christ.

We must examine our motives. We must examine our hearts, and ask ourselves, are we really saved? In the Old Testament, when somebody did something wrong, they needed to bring an offering, an animal sacrifice. They would slit the throat and shed its blood on the altar as a sin offering, then they would take the body of that animal and burn it on the altar. The shed blood and the burnt body would mediate between a holy God and a sinful creature. In Hebrews 10:15–20, in verse 19, it states,

> **Since therefore, brethren we have confidence to enter into the holy place by the blood of Jesus.**

In verse 20, we read that Jesus Christ opened up a new and living way, which he inaugurated for us through the veil, that is, his flesh.

This innocent Lamb who knew no sin became sin for us so that we, through his death, burial, and resurrection, would have access to the throne room of Almighty God and plead our case with him. Drinking his precious blood unworthy means not understanding our status positionally, that through the shed blood of Jesus, we have been purified, we have been cleansed, we have been mediated for, we have been made righteous, we have accepted him as our Savior and Lord, and we have invited him to come into our hearts, and he has come in, and therefore, we are worthy to participate of his blood in communion.

To participate of his flesh means that we understand that in Isaiah 53:4–7, he was wounded for our transgressions. He was bruised for our iniquities. A chastisement of our peace was upon him, and by his stripes we are healed.

When we repent and ask God for forgiveness and invite Jesus Christ to be our Savior and Lord, he becomes our substitutional lamb on the altar, whose precious blood is shed for us and whose body was crushed in our behalf.

So, therefore, we must confess all our sins and, at that moment of communion, ask him to cleanse us from the crown of our head to the soles of our feet with his precious blood, and also thank him that it was shed for the remission of sin and so we may have access into the holy place.

Then when we take the bread, thank him that through his flesh we have no more iniquities, no more transgressions, no more chastisement, and by his stripes we are healed. Then take the bread, put it in our mouth, and slowly remember that he was wounded in our behalf, and thereby, you will know why we are worthy to participate in Holy Communion.

Now the other part of the body that we need to acknowledge is found in 1 Corinthians 12:12–27, and that is the body of Christ, which is not just the physical crushed lamb of God sacrificed for the sin of the world, but also each individual member in the local church as members of his body, and when we hurt someone in the body, his corporate body of believers, we are hurting him, and this too we must discern.

So when you have the bread in your hand as you are participating in Holy Communion, also remember that every believer, every Christian, every blood-bought child of God is worthy of a godly treatment, respect, and honor because they are members of Christ's body, the church.

Now let's analyze our reward for being obedient to the instructions of the apostle Paul.

> **I will not be weak, I will not be sick, and definitely, I will not die.**

In verse 30, it explains it clearly, and in verse 31, it gives us the instructions so that we won't be judged, condemned, and ultimately, die.

I'm so glad that God's holy scriptures share with all of us exactly how to be strong and healthy and live a long life by not participating of the Lord's communion unworthy and sleep.

Number 9, dishonoring God, wrath of God revealed

This is found in Romans 1:16–32.

> **For I am not ashamed of the gospel, for it is the power of God for salvation to everyone who believes,**

> **to the Jew first and also to the Greek. For in it the righteousness of God is revealed from faith to faith; as it is written, "but the righteous man shall live by faith." For the wrath of God is revealed from heaven against all ungodliness and unrighteousness of men, who suppress the truth in unrighteousness, because that which is known about God is evident within them; for God made it evident to them. For since the creation of the world his invisible attributes, his eternal power and divine nature, have been clearly seen, being understood through what has been made, so that they are without excuse.**

I need to inject something here. The apostle Paul was not ashamed of the gospel of Jesus Christ, for it is the power of God for salvation to everybody who believes, to the Jew first, and also to the Greek. Notice here the only good news that human beings need. It's the good news that took place on the cross of Calvary, the sacrificed Lamb for the sin of the world, in substitution for the sin of human beings. Hear the words "power," "forgives sin," "destroys yokes," and "mediates between a holy God and a sinful creature."

This God-given power destroys the power of Satan, of all his demon powers, and liberates us from the grip of hell and the bondage that sin and Satan had over us.

For in this power, the righteousness of God is revealed from faith to faith. That is why it says, "But the righteous man shall live by faith." It is the power of God that imputes righteousness to clean, wash, and deliver a sinner. This is why the devil hates this message. This is why this message is hated in some countries of the world.

Now there is a wrath that comes upon people who suppress the truth in unrighteousness to commercialize, to ritualize, and to traditionalize people instead of preaching to them the good news, the gospel, and the unmerited favor of God through Jesus Christ's total work on Calvary. No other way to be forgiven, made righteous, and be saved.

For even though they knew God, they did not honor him as God, or give thanks; but they became futile in their speculations, and their foolish heart was darkened. Professing to be wise, they became fools, and exchanged the glory of the incorruptible God for an image in the form of corruptible man and of birds and four-footed animals and crawling creatures. Therefore God gave them over in the lusts of their hearts to impurity, that their bodies might be dishonored among them. For they exchanged the truth of God for a lie, and worshiped and served the creature rather than the Creator, who is blessed forever, Amen. For this reason God gave them over to degrading passions; for their women exchanged the natural function for that which is unnatural, and in the same way also the men abandoned the natural function of the woman and burned in their desire toward one another, men with men committing indecent acts and receiving in their own persons the due penalty of their error. And just as they did not see fit to acknowledge God any longer, God gave them over to a depraved mind, to do those things which are not proper, being filled with all unrighteousness, wickedness, creed, evil; full of envy, murder, strife, deceit, malice; they are gossips, slanderers, haters of God, insolent, arrogant, boastful, inventors of evil, disobedient to parents, without understanding, untrustworthy, and loving, and merciful; and, although they knew the ordinance of God, that those who practice such things are worthy of death, they not only do the same, but also give hearty approval to those who practice them.

We must always evaluate our lives, our thought life, our words, our conduct, our belief system, because when we do that, we will know exactly where our relationship with our heavenly Father is.

Selfevaluation is key to receiving forgiveness or deliverance, our rights, our privileges, and our health. Isn't that what we are looking for? A real, personal, and glorious relationship with our Maker through Jesus Christ our Lord. Our God is alive and well.

Jesus Christ of Nazareth is the same yesterday, today, and forever. It is important to understand that God was in Christ reconciling the world unto him, not imputing on to them their trespasses, and he has committed to us the word of reconciliation. In 2 Corinthians 5:19, our God does not want to destroy, reject, or give up on any person or turn his back on them because of sin; he wants fellowship and common union with his created beings.

We were created for community, fashioned for fellowship, and formed for a family, the family of God, the body of Christ, and to replenish the earth.

In verse 21, it states that for even though they knew God, they did not honor him as God or give thanks. They became futile in their speculations, and their foolish hearts were darkened.

There are a lot of people who behave very well, look very good, and act very nice but do not honor our heavenly Father or are not even thankful for the soul that is living within their bodies. They say, "Well, I love God my way, and I worship my God my way and have a relationship according to my way." The sad thing is that I wish this would be enough, but our God is looking to have communion and intimacy with us daily, not just when we remember.

With all this new technology, with all these new gadgets that we have in our homes and in our automobiles, we think that we are really wise. The Bible says we are professing to be wise, but the truth is we are becoming as fools. There's no real wisdom, there's no real knowledge, there's no real revelation in life apart from our heavenly Father, and then we exchange the glory of the incorruptible God for images of corruptible man and of birds and four-footed animals and crawling creatures.

No wonder so many people are in trouble, no longer believing in their heavenly Father or the gospel of the Lord Jesus Christ. And for this reason, God is giving them up to depraved minds to do those things that are not proper, and then when sickness, disease, and infirmity show up at the door, they hardly have any faith or a relationship with

God for that matter. In verse 24, verse 26, and verse 28, it says very clearly, "And God gave them over." He turned his back on them. He did not want anything to do with them anymore. This is so sad.

This is why so many Christians are sick. This is why so many unbelievers are sick. This is why so many people are sick. They know God but glorify him not as God.

These were Christians and people who knew God and had communion with God, or if they were not Christians, they must have known something about God because it says it very clearly. I don't know about you reading this book, but the last thing I want in this world is to lose my faith in my heavenly Father. He is the one that gave me a soul, and a heart, and health to enjoy. He is our Maker and our soul giver. He puts breath in our lungs, joy in our hearts, and gives us a reason for living. Life is worth living.

In verse 29–31 are the consequences of people turning their backs on our heavenly Father, not wanting to have anything to do with him nor wanting to listen to his word, nor wanting to relate to him as Abba, daddy.

At the age of twenty-six, I had everything the world calls prosperity—a beautiful home, furnishings two new cars, a beautiful swimming pool, a business, two beautiful children, company cars. But inside my heart of hearts, I was void and I was empty. I was lonely and despairing. I tried alcohol and that didn't help. I tried drugs and that didn't help. I tried womanizing and that didn't help. I tried the occult and that didn't work. I tried selling some drugs for the adrenaline rush and that didn't work, and finally I got caught and was sent to prison.

And there in that prison lonely feeling that the world had caved in called the work release center. I saw some young people going to Bible studies, and they invited me for the next three months. Every Friday night, they would invite me to go to Bible study, and finally I gave in. Obviously, I sat in the back and did not want any relationship with those Holy Rollers, and two and a half months later of Bible studies, they gave the altar call. I did not know that Jesus Christ of Nazareth had arisen from the dead and was seated at the right hand of the Father, interceding for me. What a glorious lawyer. I always saw him and understood him through religion as being crucified on the cross.

I was truly tired of sinning and carrying a load of guilt, shame, and unworthiness, and when they gave the altar call, I ran to the front, and I got on my knees. They laid their hands on my head. A warmth came over my body, and they said to me, "Repeat after me. Dear Lord Jesus, I repent of my sin, I ask you to forgive me, and to come into my heart, and make me a new person." At that time, with a void and a hole in my chest, with a vacuum choking me from the inside and out, the precious Lord Jesus came into my heart, and my void was instantly gone. Jesus Christ replaced it with himself. He came in to take up residence within me, and two weeks later, he baptized me with the precious Holy Spirit from the crown of my head to the soles of my feet, and I have never been the same person. I am a born-again Christian, hallelujah.

Why would I want to disobey the Lord? Why would I want to not believe his gospel? Why would I want to run away to other religions, to other philosophies, to other ancient religions, when I have the Son of the living God living within me, guiding me, strengthening me, delivering me daily from the oppression of the enemy, setting me free from everything that bothers me? Why would I not love him, respect him, and obey him? To God be the glory, amen.

Then I studied in Miami Christian College, then went to Trinity Agape Church, and Charles Quinn, my pastor, ordained me into the ministry in 1989. Charles and Lorie went to be with the Lord already. They had their church in Trinity Broadcasting Network Channel 45 in Miami, Florida, and they were gracious enough to see the Christ in me and proposed the ordination. Thanks to their obedience to the leadership of the Holy Spirit, Rev. Charles Quinn and twelve other pastors laid hands on me and commissioned me in the ministry to this day. I have preached his uncompromising gospel everywhere I go.

I have preached this glorious gospel for thirty years even before my ordination in the Dade County Jails without offerings. God has supplied every Bible I have brought in there, and every evangelistic meeting, every passion play, and I have seen hundreds of thousands of people give their lives to Jesus Christ and have a complete turnaround, marriages restored, homes put back together, and many lives healed by the power of the gospel of the Lord Jesus Christ of Nazareth. Why would I make him my enemy and have God give me up to reprobate mind?

I hope this book will encourage you to get on your knees and call on God in Jesus's name and ask him to cleanse you with his precious blood, to deliver you with his precious blood, to break every yoke of bondage in your life with his precious blood, to deliver you from the crown of your head to the soles of your feet from every influence, every oppression, and every tormenting power that is coming against your life, and for the Lord Jesus Christ to come into your heart and make you a new person and fill you with his precious Holy Spirit. Or if you are a child of God, just lift up both of your arms to the sky and say out loud, "O precious Holy Spirit, I welcome you into my room right now. I welcome you into my life right now. I welcome you into my home right now, and be real to me by manifesting yourself in this room and in my heart in Jesus's name, amen."

As I was saying this particular prayer, I sensed the power of the precious Holy Spirit in this room, filling this entire room. My friend, if you say this prayer out loud three or four times, you too will experience the manifestation of God's Holy Spirit in your room and in your heart.

Now in verse 26 and verse 27, we see how men and women gave up their natural desires for one another and adopted the desires that are unnatural, men with men and women with women. In today's society, that is called alternative lifestyles, but according to verse 26 and verse 27, God calls it unnatural and indecent acts. Now according to today's standards, it is called alternative lifestyles, but according to God, there is a consequence to that alternative lifestyle, and in verse 27 and receiving in their own persons the due penalty of their error. HIV.

God is the Arthur our marriage, man becomes wicked, sinful, and alienated from God, and by human beings not honoring God, and obeying his word, for healthy relationships, and natural affection one for the other, God has to give them up to a reprobate mind and to degrading passions. It is our disobedience to God's holy instruction that causes the judgment of God to come upon us.

The only one that knows everything about us is our Creator when we have fellowship with him daily through the reading of his holy Word, through prayer, through Bible studies, through going to church. And when we strive to develop a relationship with him, everything should come out beautiful, and we would have restored the original relationship God had with Adam and Eve, and once again we were created for community, fashioned for fellowship, and formed for family, the precious family of God.

If you are involved in one of these relationships previously mentioned, please always know that God loves you. God does not love your behavior. He loves the person, and if you have children, you know that your intentions for your children have always been good, to bless them, to fellowship with them, to be loved by them so that joy, peace, tranquility, and serenity may rule and reign in your home. A true father or mother that tells us that they do not want fellowship with their children is lying through their teeth. God made them male and the female to reproduce and have a family to show the love of the father and mother upon their children and raise up a healthy society. This is God's plan. This is God's doing. This is God's original intent. It's only when we break that original intent that things start falling apart. We become alienated, we become sick, and ultimately, before reaching ninety years of age, we die.

There's always help and a listening ear when we come to God in Jesus's name with a broken and contrite spirit. God says he will never despise when we confess our faults and failures, all our sins and alternative lifestyles, and tell him that we are willing to repent and turn our backs on that reckless living. Immediately while on your knees, the power of the Holy Spirit will invade your soul, and you will sense the resurrection power that I sense in this office right now. He will come upon you. Your mind will be delivered. Tormenting demons will leave, and the precious Holy Spirit will come into your heart, and you'll start fellowship with your Creator, your Redeemer, your Lord and Savior Jesus Christ of Nazareth. And your life will make a U-turn, and you'll start experiencing joy, peace, tranquility, and serenity. You will sleep like a baby because you would have developed your fellowship with your Father. Isn't that glorious? Hallelujah.

There is nothing that we can do on this earth. Even if God has turned his back on our willful disobedience, like a heavenly Father, he is ready, waiting, and able to receive us back in fellowship the moment that we repent from our ways and we renew the common union we once had with him. Now if we never had a common union with him, just say, "Lord Jesus, forgive me of my sin, cleanse me with your precious blood, make me a new creature. I bow my will to yours. Come into my heart and be my Lord and Savior, in Jesus's name, amen."

If you said that prayer, I believe you are born again, and all your sins have been forgiven. You're a brand-new creation in Jesus's name. Now all that you need is to find a Bible, study, and start reading the gospel of Matthew, Mark, Luke, and John so that you will know what took place in your life and start becoming the best Christian. Also find a Bible-believing church and join it, and this way, you will help others do the same. Amen.

It is important that we understand positionally and progressively that we are everything the Bible says that we are.

We can do everything the Bible says that we can do.

We should do what the Bible says we should do.

It is in what we should do that we make our mistakes. It is in what we should do that we fall. It is in what we should do that we come short. It is in developing our fellowship with him, it is in developing our communion with him, it is in learning how to renew our mind with the word that we make mistakes. It is in learning how to walk in the Spirit so that we won't fulfill the lust of the flesh, this is where we blow it. Now what is an imperfect Christian supposed to do?

The reason why I love my relationship with God through Christ so much is that he is not expecting perfection, only honesty, to be quick to confess my faults. Realize that under the dispensation of grace, he knew that in the development of the fellowship, in the development of the relationship, we would fall, make mistakes, and fall short of his best for us. Aren't you glad that we have entered into his rest and that we have been made the righteousness of God through faith and not through our works?

In 1 John 1:8–10, it states,

> **If we say that we have no sin, we are deceiving ourselves, and the truth is not in us. If we confess our sins, He is faithful and righteous to forgive us our sins, and to cleanse us from all unrighteousness.**

> **If we say that we have not sinned, we make him a liar, and his word is not in us.**

He is saying here that positionally, we are holy and perfect in the eyes of God, but progressively, in the development of the relationship, like any other natural son, we would make mistakes, fall short, and in some instances, lose our way. This is why he says if we have not sinned, we deceive ourselves, and the truth is not in us, so the fact that we sin in the development of the relationship is evidence that we are saved and that we are on our way.

If we confess our sins, he is faithful and just to forgive us our sins and to cleanse us from all unrighteousness. Now the situation here is imperfection, immaturity, and the development of the relationship. It is not giving you a key to willfully go and sin, only if we make a mistake, only if we fall short, only if we say or do something that is stupid or unbiblical, then we confess it right away to the Lord, and he is faithful and just to forgive, cleanse, and wash away everything that we have done. Aren't you glad that in the dispensation of grace as we are developing our relationship with our God, he understood we would make mistakes and he made provision for it through the confession of our faults? He is faithful and just to forgive us and to cleanse us from all unrighteousness. That is God's remedy for faults and failures.

Number 10, disobedience to God's word and unforgiveness.

In Ephesians 1:17–23, it states,

> **That the God of our Lord Jesus Christ, the father of glory, may give you a spirit of wisdom and of revelation in the knowledge of him. I pray that the eyes of your heart may be enlightened, so that you may know what is the hope of his calling, what are the riches of the glory of his inheritance in the saints, and what is the surpassing greatness of his**

> **power toward us who believe, which have brought about in Christ, when he raised him from the dead, and seated him at his right hand in the heavenly places, far above all rule and authority and power and dominion, and every name that is named, not only in this age, but also in the one to come. And he put all things in subjection under his feet, and gave him as head over all things to the church, which is his body, the fullness of him who fills all in all.**

My desire in this book is the same as that of the apostle Paul, that we all should pray, like the apostle Paul prayed, that our heavenly Father would give us a spirit of wisdom and revelation in his knowledge, and that the eyes of our hearts may be enlightened with the knowledge of the hope of his calling upon our lives and the riches of his glory in the inheritance prepared for the saints be manifested in our lives as we read his holy Bible for total well-being of our lives.

In Ephesians 2:1–5, it states,

> **And you were dead in your trespasses and sins, in which you formerly walked according to the course of this world, according to the prince of the power of the air, of the spirit that is now working in the sons of disobedience. Among them we too all formerly lived in the lusts of our flesh, indulging the desires of the flesh and often mind, and were by nature children of wrath, even as the rest. But God, being rich in mercy, because of his great love with which he loved us, even when we were dead in our transgressions, made us alive together with Christ (by grace you have been saved), and raised us up with him, and seated us with him in heavenly places, in Christ Jesus, in order that in the ages to come he might show the surpassing riches of his grace in kindness toward us in Christ Jesus.**

Where we formerly walked according to the course of this world, according to the prince of the power of the air, the Spirit is now working in the sons of disobedience.

We may be saved, Spirit filled, go to church, and read our Bible but may still be operating under a spirit of disobedience. There are many Christians who love the Lord but are still walking under a spirit of disobedience. People are under the impression that getting saved and going to church is all they need to do in order to please God, and they feel that they are right in the sight of God.

I have given you ten reasons why a lot of people don't get healed even when great and famous evangelists pray for them or even when they pray for themselves and don't get any results. We need to analyze ourselves if we are all obeying and abiding by God's principles in relation to him and to people. It is basically the law of sowing and reaping; what you do for others, it's what will come back to you. The law of the boomerang. If you sow love, you will reap love; if you sow hate, that is what you will reap. Our fellowship with God will change us in such a way that our fellowship with men will be pleasing to God.

That is why Romans 12:2 states,

> **And do not be conformed to this world, but be transformed by the renewing of your mind, that you may prove what is the will of God, that which is good and acceptable and perfect.**

We are not to operate according to this world system, with greed, selfishness, deception, lying, cheating, cursing, and hurting human beings. Our relationship with human beings and the way we treat them must be pleasing to our heavenly Father, or he will close the windows of heaven upon our lives in every area.

Sometimes were praying for something and the answer never comes. It is like there is silence from heaven. It's like he doesn't listen to us. I have made this mistake. I have been waiting for something from God, and my prayers were being hindered. When I pray for something and the prayer takes forever to be answer, I need to do soul-searching.

I need to ask God to reveal to me what principle of sowing and reaping I am breaking in relation to him and others. We are the ones that are always short-circuiting God's divine blessing upon our lives.

Now there's a lot more that we could talk about in these chapters and verses, but I just wanted to show the reader how easily we can all disobey God in our mistreatment of others and how that is what is stopping the blessing of God upon our lives.

There is a transformation that Christians need to go through from a child, a newborn babe in Christ, to an adolescent, to a teen, to an adult, then to an elder, and ultimately, to a leader in the body of Christ. There is a spiritual transformation that occurs when we stop being conformed to this world and start being transformed by the renewing of our minds with the word of Almighty God.

Our relationship starts when we are born again, then it is our responsibility to be transformed to a Christlike person. He is our only mirror for self-evaluation and correction. We must always remember that being born again is just the beginning, then comes the transformation by the renewing of our minds, and then the spiritual growth to the stature and the fullness of Christ that we may not be children tossed here and there by the waves and carried about by every wind of doctrine, by the trickery of men, by the craftiness in deceitful scheming (Ephesians 4:14).

(11) The continuation of number 10 is found in Mark 11:23–26.

> **Truly I say to you, whosoever says to this mountain, "Be taken up and cast into the sea," and does not doubt in his heart, but believes that what he says is going to happen, it shall be granted him. Therefore I say to you, all things for which you pray and ask, believe that you have received them, and they shall be granted you. And whenever you stand praying, forgive, if you have anything against anyone; so that your father also who is in heaven may forgive you your transgressions. But if you do not forgive,**

> **neither will your father who is in heaven forgive your transgressions."**

There is nothing that we cannot do if these words we just finished reading came from the mouth of God the Son. He can't lie. We can remove mountains, we can pray troubles away, we can get the best from God, we can call in seed for sowing, we can be healthy, anything we need. If we will just speak it, the mountain will be removed.

There is a prerequisite here. Whenever we stand praying, forgive if we have anything against anybody so that our heavenly Father can forgive us our transgressions.

Verse 26 talks about what is going to happen if we do not forgive. Our transgressions will not be forgiven; therefore, what we are asking for is never going to come, very simple.

Some people say to me, "But, pastor, I just cannot forgive them. They've done so much wrong to me. They hurt my emotions. They hurt me physically. They have physically beaten me up. How can I forgive them?" And I say to them, "You're right. It is hard to forgive in our natural strength, but when we close our eyes, we lift both of our arms to the sky and we say, 'Heavenly Father, heal my emotions, heal my memories, mend my broken heart, set me free from my emotional bondage and the traumatic physical pain these people have caused me, and give me the strength to release them to you for judgment. I let them go in Jesus's name.'"

On the authority of God's holy word, his supernatural power by the presence of the Holy Spirit will start mending you from the inside out, and you'll be able to release them.

In my culture, I see men as well as women that are hard-hearted, stubborn, and sick in every part of their bodies with arthritis all over their bodies, in their fingers, in their bone marrow, and they are bowed down as if carrying a huge load, and they are unforgiving, which carries the penalty of sickness.

They come to me for prayer in the healing lines, and I look at their bodies, and right away the Holy Spirit reveals to me that they are unforgiving. But they want their physical healing. The first thing I say to them as I lean over in their ear is, "You must forgive a mother or a father, a wife or a husband, a child or a friend, a boss or a president." I remind them that the reason why they are sick sixty percent of the time is because of unforgiveness, that it hinders our prayers, it hinders our faith, it hinders our joy, and it hinders God's forgiveness in our lives. By holding on to past offenses, we are holding on to physical sickness, disease, and infirmities.

So, therefore, they must forgive for me to lay hands on them and say the prayer of faith over them. According to James 5:14–15,

> **Is anyone among you sick? Let them call for we the elders of the church, and let them pray over him, anointing him with oil in the name of the Lord; and the prayer offered in faith will restore the one who is sick, and the Lord will raise him up, and if he has committed sins, they will be forgiven him.**

Sixty percent of all sicknesses and diseases are the by-product of an unrepentant heart, an unforgiving spirit, and a stubborn view and way about them. When you hold the offense that somebody else did against you, two things are happening: Number 1, those people are under bondage; you have not yet released them. Number 2, you are getting sick in your body and bitter in your heart, and you have tormenting demons in your head. The Bible says that stubbornness is as the sin of witchcraft, and that is not all there is to it. When you operate in stubbornness, neither will your transgressions be forgiven. Therefore, you are sick in body and tormented in your mind.

From these ten reasons or roadblocks, or obstacles, that the enemy throws our way so that we will not be healed in our bodies, healed in our emotions, healed in our minds, and walking in fellowship with our heavenly Father is where we need to analyze our communication with God, our belief system and relationship with God, or whether we are in faith or just trusting in God. This is where we need to make adjustments.

Let's analyze what we have been reading so far: (A) Jesus Christ of Nazareth was a substitutional lamb for our sin. (B) He was a mediator between a holy God and a sinful creature. (C) He was the propitiation for our sin. (D) He was a justifier for our sins. (E) He was the provider of the law of faith. (F) He gave us the power to honor the man of God. (G) He gave us the power to honor grace and never go back to our tradition. (H) He gave us two new laws. (I) He gave us communion and worthiness. (J) He liberated us from the wrath of God if we don't hold back the truth. (K) He taught us to be obedient. And (L) he taught us to be forgiving. Everything he has given us, we do not have an excuse to hold back and be disobedient to the will of God. Thank you, Lord, for what you have done.

(12) Natural reasons why people haven't received their healing.

This is found in Mark 16:14.

> **And afterword he appeared to the 11 themselves as they were reclining at the table; and he reproached them for their unbelief and hardness of heart, because they had not believe those who had seen him after he had risen.**

He reproached them for their unbelief and hardness of heart, religiosity, traditions of men, cultural beliefs, and upbringing beliefs, religions of men, and even some Christian faiths who do not believe that divine healing, and divine health, is for today, are constantly running to medical doctors to get healed, to be prescribed medicine, and even go into hospitals.

They have more faith in scientific medicine and natural doctors than in God Almighty, the Healer himself, that through Jesus Christ on the cross, he took away all our infirmities.

Well, if I get totally healed, I may lose my Medicaid Medicare benefits. Can you believe what I'm going to do with myself without those benefits?

Others say to me, "If I get totally healed, I'm going to lose all the attention my husband, or my wife, gives me. I may lose the attention of my children. My grandchildren are not going to come and see me anymore. Besides, I really enjoyed the attention. It's time for them to come and see me, and have mercy on me." This pity party and "poor old me" syndrome is another way to not get healed. This would really be funny if it wasn't so pathetic.

After thirty years of going to different hospitals and going to different homes by the bed of the afflicted and hearing these pathetic excuses, sometimes I wonder what is going on in these people's mind, and the sad thing is, they tell me they are Christians, full of the Holy Spirit. Some say, "Oh, yes, I know God can heal me." Others say, "Oh, yes, I know in his timing he will heal me." And this is the ultimate: "God is using this sickness and this disease to get me to reach the nurse and the doctor with the gospel of Jesus Christ."

Then I say to them to not receive any pills, do not get injected, do not get any intervenes, don't get healed, because if God is using you here, you will be in total rebellion against God wanting to get healed. Stay sick as long as you can so that you can talk to the nurse and the doctor long enough about Jesus Christ. Doesn't this sound totally stupid?

Others say to me, "But if I get healed, I'm going to have to change my way of life, after all, I don't work now. I'm in my home all day, enjoying television and my favorite programming, and then I will lose all my governmental benefits, like food stamps. If I get healed, I have to go to work. I have to start exercising. I have to start eating well. All this is too much to do, and then I need to start taking charge of my life."

Others say to me, "Oh, pastor, I already prayed and I know God is going to heal me." Bad concept of timing. Notice here, these people are trusting in God to do something for them tomorrow, another method of unbelief, another excuse to self-justify the reason why they don't want to get healed, or they have been prayed for and haven't gotten healed.

Double-mindedness, laziness, work, attention, self-pity, low self-esteem, low self-value, low self-worth, denial, desires, greed, selfishness, corruption, disrespect to God, disrespect to society, and disrespect to government are the reasons why they do not get anything from God.

James 1:6–8 states,

> **But let him ask in faith without any doubting, for the one who doubts is like the surf of the sea driven and tossed by the wind. For let not that man expect that he will receive anything from the Lord, being a double minded man, unstable in all his ways.**

If you are one of these people that are double-minded and with an unrepentant heart, there's hope for you, and Jesus Christ of Nazareth loves you.

Say, "God Almighty, I've been able to see myself in these verses, and I repent of my sin. Please forgive me, Lord, for taking advantage of the government, taking advantage of my families, taking advantage of my spouse, and flat out being lazy. I turn my back on all these ungodly maneuvers, and I want to make amends with everybody. Lord Jesus, come into my life and break every yoke of bondage, set me free from deception, give me a new heart, deliver my mind, and fill me with the precious Holy Spirit. From today on, I will be a new person, read your word, and be transformed by the renewing of my mind in Jesus's name, amen" (Romans 12:2).

(13) Not knowing our identity in Christ (we are somebody).

In 2 Corinthians 5:17–19, it states,

> **Therefore if any man is in Christ, he is a new creature; the old things passed away; behold, new things have come. Now all these things are from God, who reconciled us to himself through Christ, and gave us the ministry of reconciliation, namely, That God was in Christ reconciling the world to himself, not counting their trespasses against them, and he has committed to us the word of reconciliation.**

The first thing I want us to see here is that if any man, or woman, or child, is in Christ, he is a new creation. Old things passed away; behold, new things have come.

He is a new creature, or a new creation, or a new breed of human being without a prior existence. The old things passed away, and my old nature passed away. My hard heart passed away, my old way of thinking passed away, and my old way of acting passed away.

New things have come. We are regenerated human beings. We have a new heart, we have a new mind, we have a new way about us, and we need to start living a new life, a new thought life, and behaving Christlike. We are somebody doing something.

Now all these things are from God, who reconciled us to himself through Christ, but on top of it all, he gave us a ministry of reconciliation. Not only did he make us somebody new, but he also commissioned us to go into the world and help people get reconciled to God, hallelujah.

When we are reconciled to God and he makes us a new creation, we become his children and he withholds absolutely nothing from us, including healing.

When we receive Jesus Christ, we are also receiving the Father, for God was in Christ reconciling the world unto himself. If God was in Christ and Christ is in us, that is the hope of glory, then both of them, through the third person of the divine Trinity, live in us. I'm going to get you shouting now. In John 14:23–26, it states,

> **Jesus answered and said to him, "If anyone loves me, he will keep my word; and My father will love him, and We will come to him, and make Our abode with him. He who does not love me does not keep my words; and the word which you hear is not mine, but the fathers who sent me. These things I have spoken to you, while abiding with you. But the helper, the Holy Spirit, whom the father will send in my name, he will teach you all things, and bring to your remembrance all that I said to you."**

Verse 23 says that Jesus answered and said that if we love him and keep his word, we would be loved by the Father, and we will come to him and make our abode with him.

God was in Christ. When Jesus speaks, God is speaking in him. Three things he said were very powerful—that we would be loved by the Father, that both of them would come to us, and that both of them will make their abode within us. Now the first thing we need to ask is, did Jesus Christ come into our hearts? Or is he going to come into your heart? Notice here the difference between people who are trusting and the people who are believing. Do you trust? Or do you believe?

In the word "trusting," you are trusting that God will do something in the future for you, and the word "believing" is receiving what God has done for us already in the past.

In John 1:12–13, it states,

> **But as many as received him, to them he gave the right to become children of God, even to those who believe in his name, who were born not of blood, nor of the will of the flesh, nor of the will of man, but of God.**

We were born of the will of God by the new birth in Christ, a new created being, for as many as received him. In other translation it says, "For as many as received him to them gave he the power to become the sons of God, born of God, by the will of God, a spiritual rebirth."

Now getting back to the gospel of John.

> **He who does not love me does not keep my word, and the word that he speaks is not his own but the fathers.**

> **But the helper, the Holy Spirit which the father will send in my name, he will teach you all things, and bring to your remembrance everything I have said to you.**

Now it's important to understand that these passages are written for today and now, not just for the apostles of old but to the believers. We who are reading this book, are we trusting, or do we believe what the Bible says already happened?

Some people have a relationship with an outside-of-the-body God. The apostle Paul said, "Christ in me, the hope of glory." You and I can say Jesus Christ of Nazareth is in us and the Holy Spirit of God is in us. We are obedient to the words of Jesus. We are not the disobedient one. We are the ones that keep his commandments, and we are promised to be loved by the Father, and he and the Father are coming to make their abode with us. If this doesn't make you shout, what will?

If the passages in John 14:23–26 were only for the days of the apostles of old and not for us today, Jesus would not have said in verse 23, "If anyone loves me, he will keep my word; and my father will love him, and we will come to him, and make our abode with him." I rest my case. If this is not self-explanatory, what is?

In John 3:3–8, it states,

> **Jesus answered and said to him, "truly, truly, I say to you, unless one is born again, he cannot see the kingdom of God."**

Here we are talking about a born-again experience, a spiritual rebirth. When Jesus in the person of the Holy Spirit comes inside your human soul, you have a spiritual rebirth. Here Jesus is talking with Nicodemus, a religious Pharisee who knew everything there was to know about the law but did not have a spiritual regeneration; he was not spiritually made alive.

When I was born again and Jesus came into my heart, he filled the emptiness and the vacuum that I felt with his spirit, then I became a spiritually born-again Christian. This is what we all need, not just an intellectual religious communion with God, but a rebirth. We always have to go back to that first encounter we had with Jesus. Regardless of how you feel today and how far away you may think you are from him, remember your rebirth experience. Obviously, here comes human reasoning.

> **Nicodemus said to him, "How can a man be born when he is old? He cannot enter a second time into his mother womb and be born, can he?" Jesus answered, "Truly, truly, I say to you, unless one is born of water and of the spirit, he cannot enter into the kingdom of God. That which is born of the flesh is flesh, and that which is born of the Spirit is spirit."**

The difference between a religious person who trusts that God will do something for them in the future, including grant him the privilege to go to heaven, and the born-again Christian, the person who had an encounter with the Lordship of Jesus Christ, the person that invited Jesus to come into their lives, and even while being a baby they experienced the supernatural power of God, a spiritual rebirth that comes out of a person who believes, that is a spiritual person that truly believes, for as many as believed gave he power to become. Are you? Or are you not? Are you a believer? Or do you trust?

Nicodemus was a religious person, and Jesus told him that unless he was born again, he could not see nor enter the kingdom of God. Before I was born again, I could not see the spiritual realm. I could only understand the intellectual and physical realm, but when Jesus came into my heart, the eyes of my understanding were enlightened. I had a spiritual regeneration, I was able to see the kingdom of God, and I entered the kingdom of God through the rebirth.

I looked up a *Webster* dictionary, and I looked up the word "regeneration," and this is what I found: number 1, "the act of regenerating, or the state of being regenerated"; number 2, "the impartation of spiritual life by divine grace, even the secular world knows there's an impartation of divine spiritual life"; number 3, "the reproduction of a lost part or organ, as in lizards"; number 4, "the renewal or reproduction of cells, tissues, etc."; number 5, "the process by which, in the various devices, heat or other forms of energy are saved and reutilized." Now there are a few others, but I think you got the picture.

Or either we believe the word of God to be true, or we believe the word of God to be a lie. You be the judge. No wonder Jesus told Nicodemus that his religious intellectual philosophies were not enough in order to see or enter into the kingdom of God; he had to be born again.

In John 3:9–10, it states,

> **No one who is born of God practices sin, because his seed abides in him; and he cannot sin, because he is born of God. By this the children of God and the children of the devil are obviously: anyone who does not practice righteousness is not of God, nor the one who does not love his brother.**

No one who is born of God practices sin. We don't willfully practice it, but every Christian that is learning to read the Word, that is learning to develop their spiritual walk and is learning to renew their mind, that is learning to walk in the Spirit do sin by ignorance, lack of spiritual growth, lack of maturity, lack of knowledge, and lack of spiritual development, but the emphasis is in verse 9 ("No one who is born of God"), born of God, spiritual rebirth, Christ in you the hope of glory, children of the Almighty God, born of the spirit, recreated beings, brand-new creatures, loved by God, and the temple of God. We are somebody, and we are doing something.

In 1 John 4:9–12, it states,

> **By this the love of God was manifested in us, that God has sent his only begotten son into the world so that we might live through him. In this is love, not that we love God, but that he loved us and sent his son to be the propitiation for our sins. Beloved, if God so loved us, we also ought to love one another. No one**

> **has beheld God at any time; if we love one another, God abides in us, and his love is perfected in us.**

God is love. When God was in Christ reconciling the world unto himself, both of them came in us. And the God of love is in our hearts; the love of the Son and the love of the Holy Spirit is in us. God sent his Son to be the propitiation for our sin so we could be born of God, born of love, and love one another as he has loved us. If we love one another, God abides in us, and his love is perfected in us. Christ in us, the hope of glory.

In 1 John 5:1–5, it states,

> **Whoever believes that Jesus is the Christ is born of God: and whoever loves the father loves the child born of him. By this we know that we love the children of God, when we love God and observe his commandments. For this is the love of God, that we keep his commandments; and his commandments are not burdensome. For whatever is born of God overcomes the world; and this is the victory that has overcome the world-our faith. And Who is the one who overcomes the world, but he who believes that Jesus is the son of God?**

Notice the phrase "whoever believes." This is in the present tense, and if we read the Word of God ten years from now and Jesus tarries, it will still be in the present tense. Whoever believes that Jesus is the Christ, the anointed one, the son of the most high God, Emmanuelle, God with us in person, is born of God. I am trying to explain two things: Number 1, the new birth is for now, the Word of God is for now, the comforter the Holy Spirit is for now, and his commandments are for now. Number 2, a new birth and regenerate spirit is so that we can overcome the world, inside power for overcoming the world, and this is the victory that overcomes the world, our faith, the measure of faith that God put in us (Romans 12:3).

God has dealt to every man the measure of faith.

In Romans 12:3, it states,

> **For I say, through the grace given unto me, to every man that is among you, not to think of himself more highly than he ought to think; but to think soberly, according as God has dealt to every man the measure of faith.**

This teaching is about knowing the identity of the believer. According to some Pentecostal circles, they use part of this verse to keep us humble (not to think of himself more highly than he ought to think). The reason why I'm writing this book is to help us think (as we ought to think). How should we ought to think? If we read the Word of God, if we believe the Word of God, it says that God was in Christ and Christ is in us through the third person of the Holy Spirit, then we are a temple. We are a new created being, we are a new creature, we are a child of God, we are loved of God, and God and Jesus have made their abode with us.

In 1 Peter 1:23, it states,

> **For you have been born again not of the seed which is perishable but imperishable, that is, through the living and abiding word of God.**

Now we who are born of our mom and dad, the Bible calls it perishable seed, for we have been born again not only of perishable seed (mom and dad) but also of imperishable seed, which is the word of God, which is Jesus Christ. In John 1:1, it states that in the beginning was the word, and the word was with God, and the word was God. Now in verse 14, it states that the word became flesh and dwelt among us, and we beheld his glory as the only begotten from the Father, full of grace and truth. So when he says that we are born of the imperishable seed through the living and abiding word of God, we are born of the seed of God.

Now God is a spirit. Before the foundation of the world, in the Old Testament, in the New Testament, God became flesh in the person of Jesus Christ, and Jesus Christ became the word, and the word became flesh, and today, he is still the same. Jesus is the same yesterday, today, and forever. So when we hear the gospel and reason in our hearts that we need a Savior, we repent of our sin, and we ask Jesus to come into our hearts, he comes in through the power of the third person of the Holy Trinity and seals us with the Holy Spirit of promise. In Ephesians 1:13 Verse 13 in him, you also, after listening to the message of truth, the gospel of your salvation-having also believed, you were sealed in him with the Holy Spirit of promise, in verse 14 who is given as a pledge of our inheritance, with a view to the redemption of God's own possession, to the praise of his glory.

In Ephesians 4:30, it states,

> **And do not grieve the Holy Spirit of God, by whom you were sealed for the day of redemption.**

The way we aggrieve the Holy Spirit is by not believing the written Word of God, which he wrote with approximately forty men, inspiring them to write as the Spirit gave them the words. So it is important to have a Jesus inside our body's mentality rather than a God who we are trusting on to do something for us in the future. If we do not believe God's testament, God's covenant, what are we going to believe?

In John 10:10–11, it states,

> **The thief comes only to steal, and to kill, and to destroy; I came that they may have life, and might have it abundantly. I am the good shepherd; the good shepherd lays down his life for the sheep.**

Are we his sheep? Is he our shepherd? Did he give us life? Has he given it to us more abundantly? The word "life" is ZOE. Jesus is ZOE. When we received Jesus Christ, he comes to give us life and life more abundantly. The God kind of life, ZOE; that is what the word ZOE means.

You and I have been born again. We have a new life. We have the God kind of life, Zoe. The devil only comes to steal, kill, and destroy, but Jesus came to give us ZOE. Jesus Christ of Nazareth is that God kind of life because God was in Christ, reconciling the world to himself.

We are a recreated being. We are a new creature in Christ. We are a born-again believer. We have a spiritual rebirth. Our spirit is regenerate. We have passed from death unto life. We have the seed of God in us. We are children of the most high God. We are the seed of God, through Jesus Christ. The word "seed" means, house, descendant, family, lineage, posterity, new nature, new man.

In Ephesians 2:11–18, let's look at the following.

> **By abolishing in his flesh the enmity, which is the law of commandments contained in ordinances, that in himself he might, make the two into one new man, thus establishing peace. And might reconcile them both in one body to God through the cross, by it having put to death the enmity. And he came and preach peace to you who were far away, and peace to those who were near; for through him we both have our access in one Spirit to the father. So then you are no longer strangers and aliens, but you are fellow citizens with the saints and are of God's household.**

We should read the entire chapter 2. I only picked these few verses to show the reader that both the Jews and the Gentiles in Christ are a new man. We are all a new creation. We should not have any cultural differences because we're both born into a new family, a new spiritual family. God is a spirit. Through Christ, we are born of God, a spiritual rebirth, a new man. Our identity in Christ is totally solid, eternal, and forever.

In Galatians 3:28, it states,

> **There is neither Jew nor Greek, there is neither slave nor free man, there is neither male or female; for you are all one in Christ Jesus.**

In our relationship with God Almighty, there is neither Jew nor Greek. There is no distinction, neither the slave person nor the free man, neither the male nor the female, but all of us are one in Jesus Christ. We can have a relationship with the Jews and love them as our brothers, for we are all one in Jesus. Thank God for the precious blood on the cross, destroying the cultural walls that separated us by abolishing it in his flesh and making us one in him. A new nature. In 2 Peter 1:3–9, it states,

> **Seeing that his divine power has granted to us everything pertaining to life and godliness, through the true knowledge of him who called us by his own glory and excellence. For by these he has granted to us his precious and magnificent promises, in order that by them you might become partakers of the divine nature, having escaped the corruption that is in the world by lust.**

His divine power has granted to us everything pertaining to life and godliness through the true knowledge of him who called us by his own glory and excellence. His divine power has granted to us the God kind of life, God's godliness. This is in the present tense. I am not trusting to get this. I already have it; it's living within me. His name is Jesus Christ of Nazareth. He called us by his own glory, and excellence. Spiritual people, born-again people, believe what they have received, and they have it.

Religious people who have an intellectual knowledge of Jesus Christ himself are trusting in God, and there is nothing wrong with that in order to go to heaven, but in order to receive their inheritance in the saints and be heirs and coheirs with Christ, they must believe.

In Romans 8:15–17, it states,

> **For you have not received a spirit of slavery leading to fear again, but you have received a spirit of adoption as sons by which we cry out, "Abba! Father!" The Spirit himself bears witness with our spirit that we are children of God, and if children, heirs also, heirs of God and fellow heirs with Christ, if indeed we suffer with him in order that we may also be glorified with him.**

When we believed we were sealed with the Holy Spirit of promise, and for some of us we were baptized in the Holy Spirit, and the Bible says in verse 15 that we have not received a spirit of slavery leading to fear again, but we have received a spirit of adoption as sons by which we cry out, "Abba father." God's precious Holy Spirit bears witness with our spirit, and we cry from our innermost being, "Abba, Father, our Daddy, our Maker, our Redeemer, our Savior, our Baptizer, our Seal, our Zoe, God's kind of life in us," making us his children, hallelujah, hallelujah. I sense his precious Holy Spirit inside this office. I sense his supernatural power inside this office. He wants common union. He wants fellowship. We praise him, we worship him, and he is truly worthy of adoration. Hallelujah, praise his holy name.

When we believe, not when we trust, he makes himself present. God is a spirit, and they who worship him must worship him in spirit and in truth. The true knowledge of him who called us by his glorious excellence through his divine power, a divine nature, no devil in hell can take this from us. He is in us, he has baptized us, and together, we will overcome everything the enemy throws our way. Hallelujah, praise his name. You see, my brother and my sister, I don't trust God in the future. I believe God in the now. I believe God in the present. He is here in my office right now through the power of the Holy Spirit. I sense his holy presence from the crown of my head to the soles of my feet.

In Philippians 3:20–21, it states,

> **For our citizenship is in heaven, from which also we eagerly wait for a Savior, the Lord Jesus Christ; who will transform the body of our humble state into conformity with the body of his glory, by the exertion of the power that he has even to subject all things to himself.**

Every born-again believer has been sealed with the Holy Spirit of promise and is heaven bound because in verse 20, it says that our citizenship is in heaven and we are waiting for the Lord Jesus Christ to take us home, where he will transform our humble estate into conformity of his glory, our new glorified bodies.

In Colossians 1:12–13, it states,

> **Giving thanks to the father, who has qualified us to share in the inheritance of the saints in light. For he delivered us from the domain of darkness, and transferred us to the kingdom of his beloved son, in whom we have redemption, the forgiveness of sins.**

God has qualified us for the inheritance of the saints—thank God for redemption—which means God bought and paid for us by the shed blood of Jesus Christ on the cross and delivered us from the domain of darkness and transferred us into a brand-new kingdom, the kingdom of his beloved Son. Think about this for a moment. God wants us to be whole in spirit, soul, and body. He sends his only begotten Son to pay on the cross our due penalties, the righteous judgment of God demanded upon us, and by shedding this holy blood, he purchased us from the devil, his legal right upon us, given to him by Adam and Eve in the garden. That completely sets us free, breaks every yoke of bondage. And then he delivers us from a different kingdom to the kingdom of his dear Son.

Can you see it? Can't you see that we have already been delivered? When the enemy puts sickness, disease, and infirmity on our bodies, he is trespassing on God's property purchased by holy blood.

In 1 Corinthians 12:13–18, it states,

> **For by one Spirit we were all baptized into one body, whether Jews or Greeks, whether slaves or free, and we were all made to drink of one Spirit. For the body is not one member, but many.**

For by one spirit we were all baptized into one body, engrafted into one body, one kingdom, the kingdom of his dear Son. We no longer belong to the domain of darkness. We now belong and are baptized into one body, one kingdom, his new kingdom, which is his body.

> **But now God has placed the members, each one of them, in the body, just as he desired.**

Aren't we glad we no longer belong to the domain of darkness? We have all been transferred to the kingdom of God's dear Son, done by the hand of Almighty God. It was God who placed us in the body of his dear Son corporately, and we are now all members of the body.

This is real and powerful. This is something we can bank on for the rest of our lives. Now let's do a recount on all our inheritance in the saints so that we should think on the biblical way, according to the measure of faith that God dealt to us (Romans 12:3).

We have a brand-new family with God in heaven where our citizenship awaits us, and on the earth, we have God's constitution, his holy Word with all sixty-six books that guaranties us eternity. This is enough to shout and sing the hallelujah choruses. Aren't we glad our sins are forgiven and our spirit has been made alive? That we have a new life, that we have a new beginning, that we are a new creation, that we have been seeded with a divine seed, which gives us a divine new nature, that we have Zoë, the God kind of life living within us, that we are a brand-new man born into a new organism, and that we are the temple of the Holy Spirit?

If you are not yet jumping and praising the Lord and giving him glory and honor and saying, "Glory be to God in the highest, and on earth peace and goodwill and prosperity toward men," then you definitely need to get born again and be Spirit filled to appreciate everything you have been given.

Our hearts have been changed and our mind cleared up. The oppression of the enemy has no legal right on your body. Every member of your body has to be whole; your blood, your nervous system, everything there is to know about you has to align itself to the knowledge of the holy word of God. We are temples of the Holy Spirit of the living God. No unholy thing should be trespassing and coming on to God's holy temple, for we have been bought and paid for by the blood of the Lord Jesus Christ. We belong to God.

(14) Prayer the key to access

In Genesis 20:17, Abraham prayed for Abimelech.

Here we see how Abraham prayed for Abimelech, for his wife and his maids, so they would bear children, and God healed them all.

The key for health, that key to getting set free, the key to being delivered, is through prayer. In Psalms 41:1–13, we will see exactly what happened when David cried out to God in his need of deliverance and healing.

> **How blessed is he who considers the helpless; the Lord will deliver him in a day of trouble. The Lord will protect them, and keep him alive, and he shall be called blessed upon the earth; And do not give him over to the desire of his enemies. The Lord will sustain him upon his sick bed; in his illness, thou dost restore him to health. As for me, I said, "O Lord, be gracious to me; heal my soul, for I have sinned against thee." My enemies speak evil against**

> **me, "When will he die, and his name perish?" And when he comes to see me, he speaks falsehood; his heart gathers wickedness to itself; when he goes outside, he tells it. All who hate me whisper together against me; against me they device my heart, saying, "A wicked thing is poured out upon him, that when he lies down, he will not rise up again." Even my close friend, in whom I trusted, who ate my bread, has lifted up his heel against me. But thou, O Lord, be gracious to me, and raise me up, that I may repay them. By this I know that thou art pleased with me, because my enemy does not shout in triumph over me. As for me, thou dost uphold me in my integrity, and thou dost set me in thy presence forever. Blessed be the Lord, the God of Israel, from everlasting to everlasting. Amen and amen.**

Here we see a broken and contrite spirit, a person who has just sinned against God, and the first thing we see here is a totally surrendered person, totally humbled person acknowledging that he had made some poor choices in his life and asking God himself to be gracious to him and to heal his soul, for he acknowledged that he had sinned against God. Here we see the Psalmist in sickness complaining about his enemies and false friends.

If you don't understand your rights and privileges, if you don't understand God's covenant, if you don't understand God's will, if you don't understand God's testament, you definitely have to pour yourself before God. Get on your knees and call out to God, reminding God of his holy word and the shed blood of Jesus Christ on the cross and the fact that you are a member of Christ's body, that you are God's holy temple, or that you need to be saved, whatever the case may be. We always start on our knees, asking God to mend our soul and to heal our soul. Always remember that our soul has emotions, free will, and knowledge, and that we are a free moral agent.

God healed through his servants, apostles, and Spirit-filled saints of God, and he does his healings even today.

God is the healer, God is the deliverer, God is the baptizer, and God is the giver of the comforter, the Holy Spirit.

He delegates his healing power only to those who believe. In James 5:16, it states that we should confess our faults one to another and pray one for another that we may be healed; the effectual fervent prayer of the righteous man can accomplish much.

That is why it's so important to have a prayer buddy, someone you can confess your faults to, someone who is not going to judge you, one you can confide in, and preferably someone who is filled with the Holy Spirit and who believes in divine healing.

He also delegates his healing power to those he sends (Mark 16:15–18).

He also delegates his healing power to the elders of the church (James 5:14).

And it is done through the power of the Holy Spirit and the gifts (1 Corinthians 12:9) to another faith by the same spirit and to other gifts of healing by the one spirit.

We always need someone to pray over us and agree with us that the spirit of infirmity, sickness, and disease has no legal right on us and inside our body, and hopefully, he has sufficient faith to bind it, rebuke it, and command it, in Jesus's name, to flee from us, and if necessary, in faith, to ask God for a creative miracle to reproduce a new organ, setting free all the members of our body. A prayer warrior brother in Christ is one of the greatest gifts that God can give us in this life.

Now we are going to try to do something that I don't think has ever been done in any kind of a book, and that is to communicate with our heavenly Father and learn to have fellowship with him and communion with him, that is with God the Holy Spirit. And that is a twofold task. We're going to start by knowing in the scriptures what God has already done.

In James 4:5–6, it states,

> **Or do you think that the Scripture speaks to no purpose: "He jealously desires the Spirit which He has made to dwell in us"? But he gives a greater grace.**

> **Therefore it says, "God is opposed to the proud, but he gives grace to the humble." Submit therefore to God, Resist the devil and he will flee from you.**

God does not speak in his word without purpose. God jealously desires us, and he wants the spirit he has put inside us to fellowship with him. I think we have explained it very carefully that we have a born-again experience, and when we repented, turned our backs on sin, and accepted Jesus Christ of Nazareth as our Lord and Savior, God sent the spirit of his Son into our hearts, and in Romans 8:16, it states, "The Spirit himself bears witness with our spirit that we are children of God."

Because we are children of God, our heavenly Father jealously desires communion with us. He gives a greater grace to those that are humble, and he is opposed to the proud. So in these next teachings, we want to humble ourselves before God Almighty and try to analyze in our thought life, our speech life, our relationship with God, and our relationship with other people what our Christian walk is like. Remember that our goal is fellowship and common union.

So we are going to submit to God Almighty, and we're going to resist the devil, and the Bible says he will flee from us.

Three questions: Number 1, am I a skeptic? Number 2, am I a religious person? Number 3, am I a spiritual person?

(15) Not knowing how to enter God's Holy of Holies (through prayer)

In the Psalms 103:1–6, it states,

> **Bless the Lord, O my soul; And all that is within me, bless his holy name. Blessed the Lord, O my soul, And forget not none of his benefits; Who pardons all your iniquities;**

> **Who heals all your diseases; Who redeems your life from the pit; Who crowns you with loving-kindness and compassion; Who satisfies your years with good things, so that your youth is renewed like the eagle.**

This is a prayer that the Psalmist said with many rewards attached to it, and if you haven't believed anything in this book, please believe this one prayer and make it your own.

In order to enter the Holy of Holies through prayer, we must first address skeptic point of view. If you don't believe anything you have already read, that is your right, and how sad would that be that you probably purchased this book or it was given to you and after reading everything, you still don't believe. So the first thing we need to do is ask God to help you believe.

"God Almighty, I don't even know if you exist. I don't even know if you hear my prayer, but if everything I have read is true, I want Jesus in my life. I want all his benefits in my life, and I want them to pass on to my children.

Please forgive me for all my sin. I repent of my skepticism, I repent of the reckless lifestyle that I have been living alienated from God, and I ask you to help my unbelief. Lord Jesus, come into my heart and make me a new person, cleanse me with your precious blood, and make me a new creature, and right now, baptized me in the Holy Spirit of Almighty God, amen."

Friend, I believe it. You said that prayer from the bottom of your heart. You have been born again, and you will experience the most marvelous, glorious, and beautiful life ever.

Now for the religious person, and you know who you are. You have rejected everything that has to do with the baptism in the Holy Spirit and the evidence of speaking in other tongues with the gifts of the Holy Spirit operating in your life. But you're empty, you're powerless, and you know there is more to your Christian walk, but you are afraid to say anything to anybody about it. You may very well be a pastor or a religious leader in your denomination, and you have been going to church for a number of years, and you're basically hiding behind a bunch of religious dos and don'ts and denying the power of thereof.

The first thing we want to share with you is found in Acts 19:1–6.

> **And it came about that while Apollo's was at Corinth, Paul having passed through the upper country came to Ephesus, and found some disciples, and he said to them "Did you receive the Holy Spirit when you believed?" And they said to him, "No, we have not even heard whether there is a Holy Spirit." And he said, "Into what then were you baptized?" And they said, "In John's baptism." And Paul said, "John baptized with the baptism of repentance, telling the people to believe in him who is coming after him, that is, in Jesus." And when they heard this, they were baptized in the name of the Lord Jesus. And when Paul had laid his hands upon them, the Holy Spirit came on them, and they began speaking with tongues and prophesied.**

In Acts 2:39, it states,

> **For the promise is for you and your children, and for all who are far off, as many as the Lord our God shall call to himself.**

When Jesus Christ of Nazareth was accused of healing people by the power of Beelzebub in Mark 3:22–26, he said that a demon-possessed person cannot lay hands on the sick and they shall recover. He said that a kingdom divided against itself would not stand and that a house divided against itself would not stand.

So in Acts 2:39, if we are called to himself, this promise of the baptism in the Holy Spirit is for us, not just for the believers of old, but for every person who believes in the Lordship of Jesus Christ. I know because I have received him, and some of the gifts of the baptism of the Holy Spirit are operating in my own life, and I've laid hands on the sick and they have recovered. And I have prayed in the last thirty years for hundreds of people, if not thousands of people, and they have recovered. They have been healed. Recreated organs have been done in their lives. Please understand, I am not a healer. It is one of the gifts of the Holy Spirit that we previously mentioned already in this book.

I have met a lot of Christians throughout my thirty years' experience in three or four denominations who secretly come to me without their pastors knowing, asking me about the baptism in the Holy Spirit after they have believed (mentioned here in Acts 19:1–6).

And I have gently taken them through these chapters and verses that we have already read, and I have laid my hands upon their head, and I have asked the Father in the name of Jesus a simple player, just like the apostle Paul did, and they have received the second manifestation of grace, which is the baptism in the Holy Spirit.

You have had an intellectual religious relationship with Christ through his word, but you are lacking the supernatural power in order to live the Christian life, and in a moment, I'm going to lead you in a simple prayer that may very well revolutionize your walk with Christ. You have absolutely nothing to lose because Jesus said, "Ask and you shall receive, seek and you shall find, knock and it shall be opened unto you" in Matthew 7:7–12.

> **If you then, being evil, know how to give good gifts to your children, how much more shall your father who is in heaven give what is good to those who ask him!**

So I believe that the prayer that you ought to say right now should be, "Father God in Jesus's name, you said ask and you shall receive. You said that the baptism in the Holy Spirit is for those who are called to yourself. I am a believer because I have made Jesus Christ the Lord and Savior of my life, but, Lord, I am living a powerless life. I know that I have grieved you by speaking evil of the external manifestation of those who are baptized in the Holy Spirit, and I have attributed to the devil those gifts of the Holy Spirit. And for that, I ask you to forgive me and to cleanse me with the precious holy blood of Jesus. Right now, Lord, I raise both of my arms to the sky. I open my heart wide, and I call upon you, God, in the name of Jesus, baptized me with your Holy

Spirit and with power, for I surrender all my ignorance on this topic, in Jesus's name, amen."

You know as I said this prayer, I closed both of my eyes, and I

lifted up both of my arms to the sky, and I felt a supernatural warmth come all over my body and inside my body, and I felt a refreshing presence in this office.

We're going to try to enter into the Holy of Holies through prayer in a few moments.

Now let's address the spiritual person. I have no idea what your spiritual walk with Christ is, but my goal in this book is to help every reader have a spiritual encounter with God Almighty, because he said that they who worship him must worship him in spirit and in truth.

I see in a lot of circles a lot of intellectualism, a lot of physical work, and a lot of enthusiasm, but very little spirituality. Hopefully, we will address that.

The first thing we want to do is come before the Lord in Jesus's name, asking him in full assurance of faith to cleanse us and to break every yoke of bondage in every area of our lives.

Please remember that everything we do in relation to our Father in Jesus's name cannot harm us, torment us, influence us, or do any kind of evil, for every good and perfect gift comes from the Father of lights, and nothing from him can hurt us.

Let me explain some manifestations that you will experience as you grow closer to God and as you experience the baptism in the Holy Spirit with his precious anointing inside your body.

You will experience coughing. You will experience sneezing. You will experience wanting to go to the toilet. You will experience a warmth coming over your body, a tingling sensation all over your body, watery eyes, a tremendous amount of joy, a tremendous amount of deliverance, like a huge load was just lifted off your neck. You will experience light-headedness. You will experience pain going away from your head, pain going away from your throat, pain going away from your lungs, pain going away from your spinal cord, pain going away from your waist. You will experience pain going away from your chest, and you will experience a sense of renewal. And faith will rise up from within you, and you'll want to share this with everybody.

And many other parts of your life will be refreshed and renewed by the precious Holy Spirit, which will invade your soul.

Sickness, disease, and infirmity will be wiped away. Your entire body will start functioning right, and if you're seated in a wheelchair or reading this book in a bed, you'll have an urge to get up and walk in Jesus's name, hallelujah, hallelujah, hallelujah. As I speak these words, the precious Holy Spirit is all over me from the crown of my head to the soles of my feet, and I sense the resurrecting life that God used to raise Jesus Christ of Nazareth from the dead flowing through me right now. Amen.

Let's pray together.

"Heavenly Father, in the name of Jesus, I come to you right now with a troubled mind. My thought life is influence and tormented by oppressing unbiblical spirits, and I know, heavenly Father, that the born-again believer who is filled with the Holy Spirit cannot be demon possessed, only influenced and tormented. Please, heavenly Father, in the name of Jesus, cleanse me right now with the precious blood of Jesus, from the crown of my head to the soles of my feet, and deliver my mind from resentment, hatred, anger, fear, rejection, feeling unwanted, and feeling unloved. Deliver me from self-pity. Deliver me from jealousy, depression, worry. In Jesus's holy name, I pray, amen.

"Father, in the name of Jesus, destroy every yoke of bondage that is influencing, that is oppressing, that is tormenting my thought life in reoccurring unclean thoughts and acts regarding sex, which include fantasy lust, all sorts of sex experiences outside of marriage, and deliver me from unclean spirits with the precious blood of Jesus. Deliver me from masturbation, lust of the eyes, lust of the flesh, and the pride of life. In the name of Jesus Christ of Nazareth, cleanse me right now and deliver me from homosexual spirits, fornication, adultery, incest, and lesbianism, in Jesus's name.

"Heavenly Father, in Jesus's name, deliver me right now from every influence, bondage that pornography has done in my life and in my family members, and I will turn away from it, from today on in Jesus's name, amen. Father, I promise in Jesus's name to throw away all porn paraphernalia that is in my house.

"Father God, I come to you in Jesus's name, cleanse me right now with the precious blood of Jesus, and destroy all the influence and tormenting demon power that religious cults, religious error, and all sorts of spirits that have caused harm in my life found in Deuteronomy 18:9–15.

"And right now I use the blood of Jesus Christ to apply it to my mind, to my throat, to my lungs, to my back area, to my waist area. Father, I use the blood of Jesus as the children of Israel used it in the Old Testament to sprinkle it on the doorposts so that when the death angel would pass by, it would not hurt them. Right now, I apply the precious blood from the crown of my head to the soles of my feet, and I ask you, Father, to build a hedge of protection with it around this property, in Jesus's name, amen.

"Heavenly Father, in the name of Jesus Christ, I ask you to invade every particle of air that I breathe inside this house. Send forth your precious Holy Spirit and invade my living room, my bedroom, every other room in this house. Cover this entire house with your precious Holy Spirit. I want to fellowship with your Holy Spirit. You are a Holy Spirit. No unholy thing in my life is welcome. Please, Father, cleanse me from everything that will hinder the flow of the Holy Spirit in every area of my life, in Jesus's name, amen.

"Heavenly Father, I lift both of my arms to the sky, and I surrender my will. I surrender before you, heavenly Father, and I ask you to come into this room. I welcome you, Holy Spirit. You are the third person of the Holy Trinity, and I welcome you. You are God in the spirit, and they who worship you must worship you in spirit and in truth. I want to have common union with the precious Holy Spirit, so I need you to reveal to me any other area in my life, any other sin in my life, any other wrong that I might have done by ignorance or knowingly. In Jesus's holy name, I pray, amen.

"So, heavenly Father, you are the spirit, and where the spirit of the Lord is, there is liberty, and our bodies are the temple of the Holy Spirit. Right now, precious Holy Spirit, I invite you to come into my life right now. Invade my entire being, saturate my entire heart, and fill me from the top of my head to the soles of my feet. Reveal yourself to me.

"I want all the fruits of the Holy Spirit operating in me, precious heavenly Father. I want the gifts of the Holy Spirit flowing through me for the common good and for ministry's sake. Oh, precious heavenly Father, have mercy on every area of my life that does not please you and teach me your ways, for I am tired of being carnal. I want to start walking and be led by your Holy Spirit. This way, I will not fulfill the lust of the flesh. My greatest desire is to have fellowship with you, Father, and have communion with you. I worship you, Jehovah God. I give you honor and praise and adoration, for you are worthy of it all, Father, in Jesus's name.

"Heavenly Father, teach me to recognize the voice of the Holy Spirit from the voice of human reasoning, from the voice of the flesh, from the voice of demonic power. I know I was created for fellowship, and that is what I want. Holy Spirit, you said that the letter kills but the Spirit gives life, and that is what I want, precious Holy Spirit—life, and life abundant, in Jesus's name, amen.

"Father, as I open my heart. I invite the precious Holy Spirit to invade my soul right now. Come now, precious Holy Spirit. Come into my heart right now and invade every part of my life, in Jesus's name, amen and amen."

We must understand that God in the person of the Holy Spirit is like a person. He has feelings, he has knowledge, he can be grieved, he can be lied to, he can be rejected, and he feels when he is not welcome. This is why it is important that when we raise our hands to the sky and we call upon the precious Holy Spirit, no sin, no rebellion, no spirit of disobedience, no flesh contamination with demoralized acts should be present because he is a holy spirit, and without holiness, no one will have fellowship with the Lord.

I see so many brothers and sisters in Christ who have secret sins in their lives, who are gluttonous, who are being driven by the lust of the eyes and the lust of the flesh. And I look at their eyes, and I hear them speak, and it's amazing the things that come out of their mouth. It is amazing to see them behave, and that should not be. We should be Christlike; we should strive for maturity to the stature and the fullness of Christ.

I encourage you to read 1 Peter 2:11–25, and read it carefully, because in order to receive anything from God, and especially in the area of divine healing or divine health, our thought life, our speech life, and our conduct has a lot to do with it. Our obedience to the precious word of Almighty God in this epistle of Peter will assure us that living as servants is the perfect will of God for our lives. I encourage you not to give up on your heavenly Father, because we have been made in his image and likeness, and he has redeemed us from the curse of the law and from the bondage of sin and has set us free to live abundantly the Christian life.

My prayers to God, in Jesus's name is, that this material you are now reading would inspire you, cleanse you, deliver you, and open the eyes of your understanding to the fullness of the grace of God in Christ Jesus. And let your spirit man, your soul man, and your body be completely healed and preserved blameless to the coming of the Lord, in Jesus's name.

Hallelujah, hallelujah, praise the holy name of Jesus. Thank you, Father, for being alive and well and having your resurrected Son sitting at your right hand, interceding day and night for everyone that is reading the holy scriptures, God's holy Word, and that everyone reading this book will sing praises and share their results with everyone they know, in Jesus's holy name, I pray, amen.

I encourage you to take your inheritance by faith right now, and get up and do something you were not able to do before. Get up and walk. Get up and bend over. Do something different because faith without works is dead (James 2:17). You must do something even if you didn't sense anything, which I truly doubt at this point, but do something. Try to move, raise both of your arms to the sky, move them back and front, up and down, and you will experience how the pain is going away. All your sinus pain, all your headaches, all your pain might have already disappeared, but keep confessing that by his stripes you are healed.

"By his stripes, I have been healed. Redemption is mine. I am set free. I am a child of the most high God, and by the stripes of Jesus Christ, I have been made whole, in Jesus's name, amen."

It may take ten minutes, it may take two hours, or it may take two days. Keep confessing it and believing it in your heart, and it's yours. May God richly bless you and all your family members. Amen.

About the Author

Rev. Pablo Arocha is an evangelist for the body of Christ, a father, a grandfather, an author, an inventor, and a motivational speaker, with a calling on his life to evangelize the world by bringing revival.